Guide to the Flags of the World  S0-BSB-539

AY 1 3 1993

GUIDE TO THE FLAGS OF THE WORLD

Mauro Talocci

Revised and updated by Dr. Whitney Smith
Director, Flag Research Center, Winchester,
Massachusetts, U.S.A.

Illustrations by
GUIDO CANESTRARI
CARLO GIORDANA
PAOLO RICCIONI

Translated from the Italian by
Ronald Strom

QUILL/105 Madison Avenue/New York, N.Y. 10016

Copyright © 1977 by Arnoldo Mondadori Editore S.p.A., Milano
Translation copyright © 1982 by Arnoldo Mondadori Editore S.p.A., Milano

First published in the U.S.A. by William Morrow and Company, Inc.

Originally published in Italian in Italy in 1977 by Arnoldo Mondadori Editore under the title *Guida Alle Bandiere di Tutto il Mondo*.

Library of Congress Cataloging in Publication Data

Talocci, Mauro.
  Guide to the flags of the world.

  Translation of: Guida alle bandiere di tutto
il mondo.
  Bibliography: p.
  Includes index.
  1. Flags. 2. Heraldry. I. Canestrari, Guido.
II. Giordana, Carlo. III. Riccioni, Paolo.
IV. Smith, Whitney. V. Title.
[CR101.T3413. 1982b]   929.9'2   81-17744
ISBN 0-688-01103-9   AACR2
ISBN 0-688-01141-1 (pbk.)

Printed and bound in Italy by Officine Grafiche di Arnoldo Mondadori, Editore, Verona

First Quill Edition

1 2 3 4 5 6 7 8 9 10

Contents

Introduction

Flags are an everyday object, yet the vast majority of people are quite ignorant of them. While most individuals can recognize a half dozen national flags, generally little or nothing is known of their history, symbolism, or usage. Adults as well as children are attracted by the bright colours and motion of flags, but rarely is consideration given to why flags are used or what they mean.

The modern world is divided into independent territories which we call states. Most of these are also nations—that is, they are composed of people who think of themselves as being part of the same group, usually because of common language, religion, political traditions, ways of life, economic systems, etc. These nation-states determine the lives (and deaths) of individuals through their ideologies, production and distribution systems, and the wars they fight (and don't fight), and in countless other ways great and small. Each of these nation-states has one or more flags: those flags are the explicit outward expressions of how the country looks at itself.

Flags are used in formal and informal situations to proclaim the existence of the nation-state. Border guards, embassies, parading soldiers, platforms for official ceremonies, and hundreds of other circumstances manifest the existence and importance of the state through the display of its flag. The flag is a reminder of lost territories, of patriot heroes, of hopes for a better future, of the promises of religions and political systems, of the sanctity of the ways of past generations.

The more the symbolism of flags and the way they are put to use are studied, the clearer it becomes that they are in fact a system of communication. Like the signature or clothing of a person, a flag is a statement made in nonverbal terms which—if read properly—can tell us a great deal about the bearer. It is not surprising that almost without exception in the dozens of states that have gained independence since World War II, freedom has been heralded by the hoisting of a new national flag. Inclusion of that flag in front of the United Nations building in New York City is the symbolic equivalent of being recognized as a real country.

Other symbols of course exist also. The coats of arms used on diplomatic offices, official documents, coins, and other circumstances are the most important. These arms tend to have even more symbolic details which communicate information about the country than flags, but they are more restricted in usage and therefore less familiar.

Flags have been used for thousands of years. Indeed almost every society in which people live under urban conditions has had flags or vexilloids (flaglike objects), the vast majority of which have had religious or military significance. In the last few centuries flags have also been used for political parties, commercial enterprises, and signalling purposes (e.g. on boats). The national flag is a rather recent development.

The American Revolution of 1775–1783 and the French Revolution of 1789 in large part created the modern sense of citizen participation in the formation of the nation which nowadays we take for granted. At that point flags made a dramatic change from being exclusively the privilege of the ruling classes (kings, soldiers, priests) to becoming symbols of common women and men. In some countries even today it is unusual to find the national flag flown on private homes, but in most nations—even the poorest ones—people feel that the flag belongs to them and express this by flying it.

Both colours and symbols have meaning, alone and combined. These meanings, however, are not eternal inherent symbolisms but ideas which have been attributed to them officially or through long usage.

Certain themes are common: red frequently stands for revolution or courage or the heroes of liberation. Green is for hope, agriculture, the Islamic religion. Black is for the oppressive days of the past or the common bond of African heritage. There are also standard patterns of flag design by which most flags can be organized. A plain background with a central design is typical of many countries; others use stripes (horizontal, vertical, or, less commonly, diagonal), a plain or striped field with a rectangle in the upper hoist corner (known as a canton), or a flag divided in quarters, usually by a cross.

Coats of arms sometimes follow the traditions of heraldry. This was developed in the Middle Ages in Europe as a way of distinguishing the ruling classes and their property, but the artistic principles of heraldry have now become almost universal. Most coats of arms are symmetrical or at least organized around a central emblem. In addition to a shield (or circular design area), there are supporters, a crest, a motto, an encircling wreath, and a compartment or other base. (Special terms are defined in the glossary on pages 260–263.) Fierce animals and weapons suggest defense of the nation-state, while its natural riches are featured in other coats of arms.

The world of flags is constantly changing. The United States has had twenty-eight versions of its national flag, collectively documenting the growth of the nation from thirteen states to fifty. Revolution and civil war are reflected in the thirteen different flags Afghanistan has used since the beginning of the century. The revolution in Iran in 1979; the unification of the former East and West Cameroons; the change of name from Congo to Zaire; and the transition from a ministerial to a presidential regime in Sri Lanka have all been the occasion for changes of national flag design.

For those who know how to read them, flags and coats of arms provide a wealth of information. It is the object of this book to present a systematic and comprehensive overview of these symbols and their meanings. Whole books can be (and have been) written about the history and symbolism of certain national emblems, but it is also possible to compress the basic details into a handbook covering all nations. Those who wish more information are advised to obtain the books listed in the bibliography.

Interested readers may also write to the Flag Research Center (Winchester, Mass. 01890 U.S.A.), which is the leading institution in the world for collecting and disseminating data about flags and other symbols. It publishes the bimonthly *Flag Bulletin* and serves as a secretariat for the International Federation of Vexillological Associations. That organization sponsors an International Congress of Vexillology every two years when men and women interested in flags gather for lectures, tours, films, and exchange of information.

Vexillology (from *vexillum*, the Latin word for flag) is a science in the making. The term itself dates from 1957 and suggests the serious, scholarly approach which is now being taken towards the understanding of flags. While flag-waving patriots and flag hobbyists have greater numbers, the vexillologists of the world are forging the most progress, digging out facts about flags in order to make this aspect of human society better understood.

WHITNEY SMITH

Flag Research Center
Winchester, Mass.

Terminology

At the end of this book there is a glossary of special words relating to flags and coats of arms. It is important, however, that the reader note in particular the different kinds of national flags shown.

In some countries one design is used as a national flag for all purposes. Elsewhere there may be three or more flags, each with distinct uses but all serving as national flags. Vexillologists categorize them as follows:

Civil flag:	flown by private citizens on land.
State flag:	flown on public buildings on land.
War flag:	flown on military buildings on land.
Civil ensign:	flown on privately owned vessels, such as yachts, freighters, cruise ships, and fishing craft.
State ensign:	flown on unarmed government vessels, such as postal and customs vessels.
War ensign:	flown on warships.

Europe

Iceland

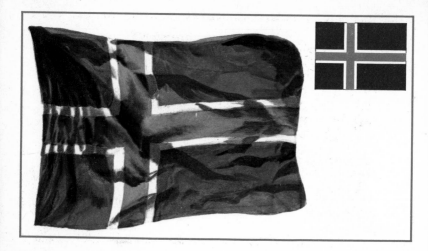

Formerly an independent state under the Danish crown, Iceland achieved de facto independence in 1941 and established a republican government in 1944.

The traditional colours of Iceland, white and blue, are those of the civil flag adopted in 1915. The typical cross reflects Iceland's place in the Scandinavian cultural area. The state flag, which is also used by the armed forces, is swallow-tailed, a form that is frequent in Scandinavia.

The national coat of arms, on a base representing part of the rocky coast, includes a bull, a vulture, a dragon, and a giant, the island's four legendary protectors which appear in the *Heimskringla*.

State arms

Presidential flag

State flag and ensign; war flag and ensign

Norway

Since the fourteenth century, Norwegian flags have reflected fundamental historical events. Norway's long subjection to Denmark (1397–1805) was reflected in the *Dannebrog*, the Danish flag. When Norway was united with Sweden, the Norwegian lion was introduced into the national flag. In 1821 a new flag was developed by laying a blue cross over the white *Dannebrog*

cross, and this flag is still used by independent Norway.

The royal coat of arms has a golden lion surrounded by the collar of the Order of St. Olaf. The lion has a crown and holds St. Olaf's battle-axe, symbols that were introduced in the thirteenth century.

Some government agencies have their own emblems on the state flag, which is swallow-tailed.

Royal arms

State arms

Royal standard

State flag and ensign;
war flag and ensign

Counties of Norway

Hordaland

Vestfold

Vest-Agder

Aust-Agder

Østfold

Buskerud

Troms

Nordland

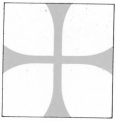

Nord-Trøndelag

Finnmark

The present Swedish flag was adopted in 1906, one year after the separation from Norway. A similar flag had been used, however, by Gustav I in the sixteenth century. The colours date from an earlier period. They probably derive from the three gold crowns on a blue field which have constituted Sweden's coat of arms since the fourteenth century.

The cross and the swallow tail of the Swedish war flag and ensign reflect the bonds that unite Sweden with other Scandinavian and Baltic countries.

Greater state arms

Lesser state arms

Royal flag

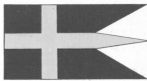

War flag and ensign

Finland

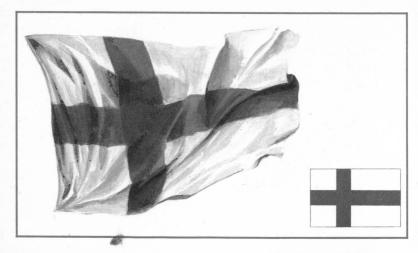

Finland was subject to Sweden until 1808 and then to Russia. In 1917 it became independent. The colours of the flag, originally adopted in 1918 and most recently modified in 1978, are white and blue, symbolizing snow and sky. The present coat of arms is almost identical with the one that was granted to Finland in the sixteenth century when it became a grand duchy. When Finland became a republic, the ducal crown over the shield was removed.

The Åland Islands, an autonomous county of Finland, have their own flag, which can be flown on land but not at sea.

State arms

Presidential flag

War flag and ensign

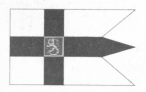

State flag and ensign

Åland Islands

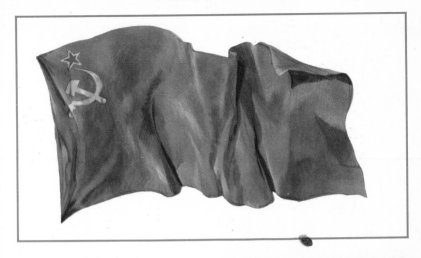

The flag of the USSR, the first country to have a Communist government, was adopted in 1923. The flag was designed to represent the ideals of the October Revolution. The five-pointed star symbolizes the unity of the peoples of five continents. The hammer and sickle represent the workers and the peasants. The association of the colour red with revolution dates to earlier times. The present USSR flag, which was adopted in 1955, is similar to the one of 1923. In the meantime its symbols have been adopted by many other socialist countries.

Traces of the white-blue-red tricolour of tsarist Russia still survive in the war ensign and in flags of some of the Union Republics.

The international character of Communism is emphasized in the coat of arms. In addition to the star, hammer, and sickle, the earth is depicted with the rising sun, symbolizing the dawn of a new era. The motto "Proletarians of All Lands,

State flag; civil ensign

State arms

19

Union of Soviet Socialist Republics

War flag

War ensign

Unite'' is repeated in the fifteen languages of the USSR on the ribbon that surrounds the ears of grain.
Since the late 1940s, the constituent republics have adopted more individualistic flags than they had before.

The earlier flags differed from each other only in the initials of the republic, which were shown in gold on a red field.

Republics of the Soviet Union

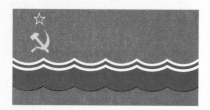

Russian S.F.S.R.

Kazakh S.S.R.

Estonian S.S.R.

Latvian S.S.R.

Lithuanian S.S.R.

Belorussian S.S.R.

Republics of the Soviet Union

Moldavian S.S.R.

Ukrainian S.S.R.

Georgian S.S.R.

Armenian S.S.R.

Azerbaijan S.S.R.

Turkmen S.S.R.

Uzbek S.S.R.

Tadzhik S.S.R.

Kirghiz S.S.R.

Ireland

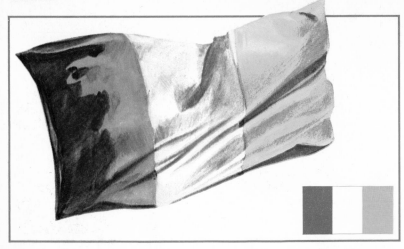

The Irish Free State was born in 1921. In 1937 a new constitution gave Ireland its own president within the Commonwealth. In 1949 it became a republic. The Irish tricolour was used as early as 1830 and was modelled on that of the French Revolution. The colours green, white, and orange were arranged in varying sequence until the 1920s, when the present order was established. It was officially confirmed in 1937.

The green symbolizes the Emerald Isle and its Catholic population. The orange symbolizes the Protestants and comes from the colour of the House of Orange-Nassau. White symbolizes the desire for peace between Catholics and Protestants.

The harp has been an Irish symbol at least since the fifteenth century, but it is not known why the symbol was originally adopted.

State arms

Presidential flag

United Kingdom of Great Britain and Northern Ireland

Royal arms

Royal flag

The Union Jack consists of superimposed crosses of St. George, St. Andrew, and St. Patrick, the patron saints of England, Scotland, and Ireland, respectively.

St. George's cross, red on a white field, was adopted by the English at the end of the thirteenth century. This symbol was carried during the wars against the Welsh and during the Seventh Crusade. St. Andrew's cross supposedly was known as early as the eighth century, but this white saltire on blue became the Scottish banner only in the thirteenth century. The union of the kingdoms of Scotland and England under James I led to the creation of the first Union Jack in 1606. The so-called St. Patrick's cross, red on a white field, was originally that of the Fitzgerald family. When Ireland was raised to the status of a kingdom in 1801, St. Patrick's cross was added to the flag. The quarter of the royal arms and the quarters of the royal shield show the

23

United Kingdom of Great Britain and Northern Ireland

three lions adopted by Richard I late in the twelfth century; the rampant lion of Scotland, which was used in the thirteenth century on the seal of Alexander II; and the Irish harp, whose origin is not known with certainty.

The use of three ensigns at sea—red, blue, and white—goes back to the time when the Royal Navy was divided into three squadrons. Nowadays the Red Ensign is flown by merchant ships, the White Ensign is reserved for the Royal Navy, and the Blue Ensign is flown by some merchant ships commanded by reserve officers, some yacht clubs, and unarmed government ships.

Blue Ensign (state ensign)

White Ensign (war ensign)

Red Ensign (civil ensign)

Regions of the United Kingdom

Scotland

Northern Ireland

Wales

Jersey

Isle of Man

Guernsey

Although the *Dannebrog* became the official Danish national flag on land only in 1854, it may be one of the oldest flags in the Western world. Legend has it that the *Dannebrog* came down from heaven to Valdemar II during his campaign against the Estonians on June 15, 1219.

The state flag, which is swallow-tailed, is also used by the army and navy, while the civil flag is displayed by private citizens.

The national coat of arms, which also appears in the royal arms, dates to the twelfth century.

Royal arms

State arms

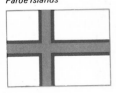

Faroe Islands

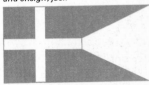

*State flag; war flag
and ensign; jack*

25

France

The French Tricolour was used for the first time in 1794 during the French Revolution. It is one of the most important flags in history because its message of liberty was an inspiration to many countries throughout the world.

It is believed that the colours are those of the city of Paris, blue and red, and of the House of Bourbon, white. But these colours go back to an earlier period of French history. St. Martin's cloak was blue, and white was associated with Joan of Arc. The oriflamme of St. Denis was red, and so was the imperial flag of Charlemagne.

The Tricolour was adopted officially in 1794, and it has been modified several times since. On two occasions at least, attempts were made to replace it altogether. During the revolution of 1848 and the Commune of 1871, a simple red flag was proposed as a national flag. For a few days in 1848 the red band was set between the blue and white bands.

Prime minister's flag

Presidential flag

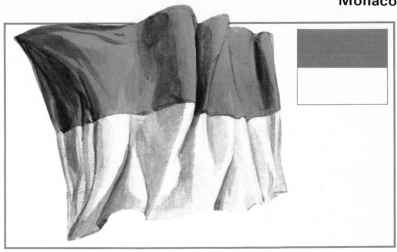

The earliest evidence of the use of white and red in the flags of the principality of Monaco goes back to the fourteenth century. Thus the bicolour that was officially adopted in 1881 as the civil ensign has deep roots in the country's history.

The lozenge design of the national colours in the coat of arms was originally used as the Monegasque flag. The motto *Deo juvante* ("With God's Help") and the two monks brandishing swords refer to a tradition of the reigning Grimaldi family. It is said that they once disguised themselves as monks and carried their swords under their tunics to capture a castle.

The personal flag of Prince Rainier is white charged with his monogram and a crown.

It is interesting to note that except for their proportions the flag of Monaco and the flag of Indonesia are identical.

State and war flag and ensign

Prince's arms

Belgium

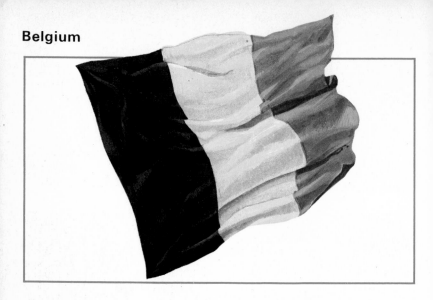

The Belgian tricolour was modelled after that of France. The colours date to 1789, but the flag was adopted officially only in 1830 when Belgium became an independent kingdom. The national colours come from the coat of arms of the duchy of Brabant and are also used in the civil ensign and in the jack. The war ensign includes a crown, two crossed cannon, and an anchor. The royal

Royal and state arms

Royal flag

Belgium

National flag on land

War ensign

State ensign

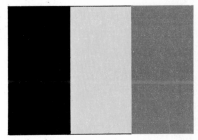

Civil ensign

standard bears a rampant lion, the coat of arms of the royal house, and, in the corners, the royal crown and the king's initial.

The crown, the lion, and the motto *L'union fait la force* ("Unity Gives Strength") are the basic elements of the royal and national coat of arms. Flemish and Walloon regional flags of the Flemish- and French-speaking portions of the population are also used.

Provinces of Belgium

West Flanders

Antwerp

East Flanders

Provinces of Belgium

Brabant

Limburg

Liège

Hainaut

Namur

Luxembourg

Wallonia

Flanders

Luxembourg

The tricolour of Luxembourg differs from that of the Netherlands in proportions and in its lighter shade of blue. The flag has been in use since the nineteenth century, but it was adopted officially only in 1972.

The flag's heraldic origins are evident from the thirteenth-century flag of Henry VI and the traditional red lion on a field of white and blue stripes. Nevertheless, the immediate aim of the choice of colours of the modern flag was to do homage to the ideals of the French Revolution.

Greater state arms
Lesser state arms

Civil ensign; aviation flag

Grand ducal flag

31

Netherlands

The rebellion of the Protestant provinces of the Low Countries against Catholic Spain succeeded in 1579 under the leadership of William I, prince of Orange and count of Nassau. The flag that was introduced then was a tricolour, orange, white, and blue.

The orange later became red, and this change was officially sanctioned in 1937. This modification may have been inspired by Dutch protest against the absolute power of the House of Orange.

Prince William's oath (*Je maintiendrai,* "I Will Maintain") appears in

Royal and state arms

Royal flag

the coat of arms together with a rampant lion holding a sword and arrows, an old emblem of Holland and the House of Nassau. The royal standard, introduced in 1908, is orange charged with a blue cross, the colour of Nassau. The horns in the quarters are those of the House of Orange.

Provinces of the Netherlands

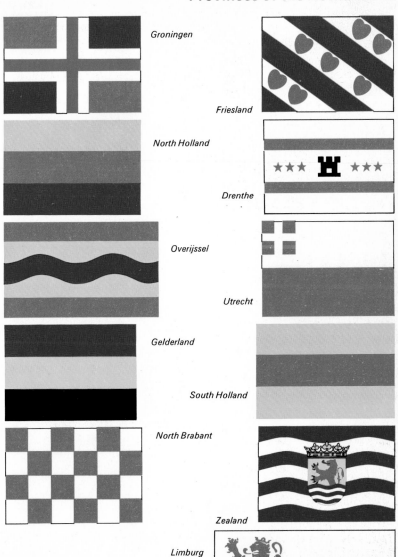

Groningen

Friesland

North Holland

Drenthe

Overijssel

Utrecht

Gelderland

South Holland

North Brabant

Zealand

Limburg

German Federal Republic (West Germany)

The West German tricolour, which was officially adopted in 1949, is directly related to the flag of the Weimar Republic. The colours black, red, and gold were long associated with pan-Germanic aspirations, and were used in the early nineteenth century in the uniforms of Baron von Lützow's famous *Freikorps*. The colour red was recurrent in the flags of the Hanseatic cities.

The black eagle in the federal coat of arms dates back ultimately to the symbol of authority of the Holy Roman Empire. The war ensign, like those of most of the countries on the Baltic coast, is swallow-tailed.

State arms

Presidential flag

War ensign

State flag and ensign; war flag

34

Länder of the German Federal Republic

Schleswig-
Holstein

Hamburg

Bremen

Lower
Saxony

Berlin

North
Rhine-
Westphalia

Hesse

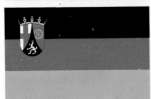
Rhineland-
Palatinate

Saar

Bavaria

Baden-
Württemberg

German Democratic Republic (East Germany)

The German Democratic Republic was established in 1949, and until 1959 it used a black, red, and gold tricolour like that of the Federal Republic of Germany.

The state emblem is shown on the flag to distinguish the East German flag from that of West Germany. The symbols that appear in the emblem are wheat, a hammer, and a pair of compasses for peasants, workers, and science and industry. The red disk represents the Communist ideology of East Germany.

A laurel wreath appears in the coat of arms of the war flag and war ensign.

State arms

Flag of the chairman of the State Council

War flag

Ensign

Poland

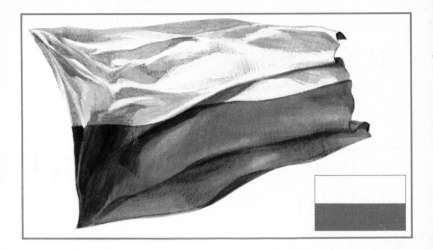

Polish flags have always been red and white, and these colours are represented in the state coat of arms. The eagle, which has been a Polish symbol since the thirteenth century, is white and the shield is red. Poland became free again after World War I and adopted a simple white and red bicolour, which is still used today.

The state and civil flag, charged with the state coat of arms on the white band, is used by the merchant marine, and the war ensign is swallow-tailed.

State arms

Civil and state ensign

War ensign

Presidential flag

37

Czechoslovakia

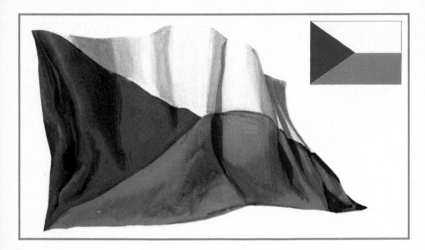

The Czech flag was adopted in 1918 and modified to its present form in 1920. The arrangement of the colours is unusual. The white and the red of the Bohemian coat of arms were adopted during the revolutionary movements of the nineteenth century. The blue is one of the colours of Slovakia (together with white and red); it became part of the new flag in 1920.

In the coat of arms the silver lion with its double tail on a red ground is traditionally ascribed to Frederick Barbarossa. Barbarossa is said to have chosen this emblem in recognition of the Bohemian soldiers who played such an important part in the conquest of Milan in 1158. The shield on the lion's shoulder represents Slovakia, with a flame of liberty against a symbol of the Carpathian Mountains.

The national motto is *Pravda vítězi* ("Truth Is Victorious").

Presidential flag

State arms

38

A contemporary chronicler relates that the urgent need to unite the Helvetic armies under one banner was met in 1339, at the Battle of Laupen, when all the soldiers were "marked with the Holy Cross, a white cross on a red shield, because for them national freedom was as sacred a cause as the liberation of the Holy Land." A similar flag was in use in the canton of Schwyz as early as the thirteenth century.

Although the individual cantons continued to use their own flags, this national banner became more and more popular, especially on the battlefield. It was adopted officially in 1848, together with a new federal constitution, and modified in 1889.

The civil ensign is flown on the lakes and navigable rivers.

State arms

Civil and state ensign

39

Swiss cantons

Aargau

Schaffhausen

Jura

Basel City

Thurgau

Basel State

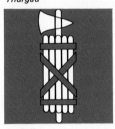

St. Gallen

Appenzell Ausser-Rhoden

Solothurn

Appenzell Inner-Rhoden

Zürich

Zug

Lucerne

Schwyz

Glarus

Obwalden

Fribourg

Nidwalden

Neuchâtel

Berne

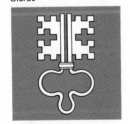

Uri

Graubünden

Vaud

Geneva

Valais

Ticino

41

Liechtenstein

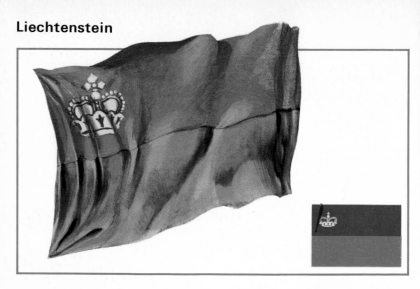

The origins of the national colours of Liechtenstein, blue and red, are not known, but they have been the official colours of the principality since the nineteenth century. The princely crown was added to the flag in 1937.

Blue stands for the sky and red for the fire of the hearth, while the gold of the crown symbolizes the unity of purpose of people and ruler. The dynastic colours, yellow and red, appear in the prince's standard and in the shield of the coat of arms. The quarters represent the descent of the reigning family, with Silesia, the Kuenrings, the duchy of Troppau, and the county of Rietberg, together with the hunting horn of Jägerndorff. When the flag is displayed vertically, which is not infrequent, the axis of the crown is parallel to the line dividing the two colours.

Prince's arms

Prince's flag

Austria

State arms

The red-white-red flag was already in use in the late eighteenth century, but it was modified after World War I when Austria became a republic. The present flag dates from 1945. During the period when Austria was annexed to Germany (1938–1945), the Nazi swastika was used.

The main element of the coat of arms, which is represented on the state and war flags, is the traditional Austrian eagle. This ancient symbol of empire was formerly two-headed and bore the shields of dependent states on its wings. The present coat of arms also includes a civic crown, a sickle, and a hammer, symbolizing the middle class, farmers, and workers, respectively. The broken chain refers to the freedom Austria regained in 1945.

State flag and ensign; war flag

43

Austrian *Länder*

The *Länder* flags are all bicolours except for Carinthia, which is a tricolour. Salzburg, Vorarlberg, and Vienna share the same flag, red on white.

Salzburg

Lower Austria

Upper Austria

Vorarlberg

Vienna

Tyrol

Carinthia

Styria

Burgenland

Hungary

The first evidence of the combination of the colours red, white, and green goes back to 1608 and is connected with the coronation of Matthias II. The individual colours go back even farther in Hungarian history. Red seems to have been the colour of the flag of Prince Arpád, who settled in the present territory of Hungary in the late ninth century. White is associated with St. Stephen I, a supporter of Christianity and the first king of Hungary. Pope Sylvester II supposedly gave the king a white cross. Green was one of the colours of the national arms in the fifteenth century.

The horizontal tricolour was influenced by that of the French revolution. The tricolour was adopted officially in 1848, and the coat of arms has been modified several times since then. In 1957 it was established in its present form.

In the present coat of arms, the ears of grain symbolize agriculture, the basis of the country's economy. The red star, a symbol of Communism, was also used by Béla Kun's short-lived socialist republic from March to July 1919.

State arms

Romania

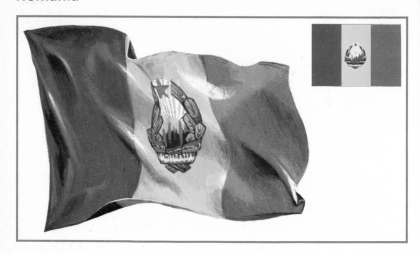

The historical flags of Transylvania, Moldavia, and Walachia are probably the source of the Romanian blue, yellow, and red tricolour, and thus their origin is heraldic.

The flag, most recently modified in 1965, had already been used in 1848 and was accepted in 1859.

The state emblem was introduced after the constitution of 1948 and was altered in 1952 and again in 1965. The mountainous landscape, the oil rig, and the ears of grain describe the physical aspect of the country and some of its natural resources. The rising sun represents the dawn of a new era; the red star refers to the country's Communist faith.

State arms

Flag of the heads of government and of state

Portugal

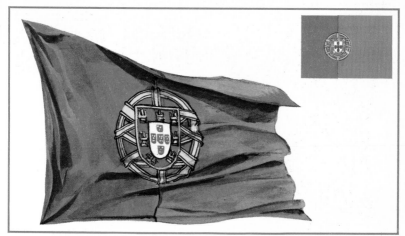

King Manuel II of Braganza was deposed in 1910, and Portugal became a republic. The following year a new flag replaced the blue and white bicolour. The colours of the new flag, green and red, were related to events that led to the downfall of the monarchy.

The great discoveries of the Portuguese navigators are commemorated in the armillary sphere behind the shield on the coat of arms. The seven castles on the red shield refer to the expansion of the frontiers of the nation carried out by Afonso Henriques. His legendary victory over five Moorish princes at the Battle of

State arms

Ourique is commemorated in the five blue shields. Each blue shield has five bezants symbolizing Christ's wounds and thereby alluding to the fact that Afonso defeated the Moors in Christ's name and with His help.

War flag

Presidential flag

47

Spain

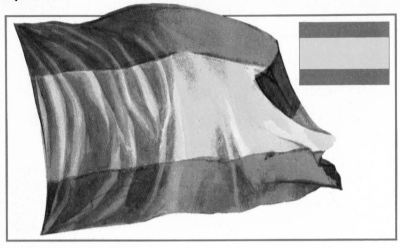

State arms

Red and gold were chosen in 1785 as Spain's colours, their heraldic origin documented by the elements in the coat of arms. The present civil flag of Spain was officially adopted in 1936, the state flag in 1981.

In the particularly elaborate coat of arms, represented by the quartered shield, are the old kingdoms of Castile (a yellow tower on a red background), León (a purple lion on a white background), and Navarre (a yellow chain arranged as a cross, saltire, and orle with a green gem at its center on a red background). At the base of the shield is the pomegranate of Granada. The "Pillars of Hercules" were originally accompanied by the motto *Non plus ultra*, later modified, after the discovery of the New World to *Plus ultra* ("More Beyond"). The dexter is ensigned by an imperial crown, the sinister by a royal crown, both coloured like the royal crown over the shield.

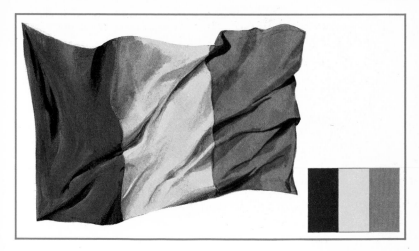

This small area in the eastern Pyrenees has been a separate state since 1278. Its sovereignty is guaranteed by the joint authority of the French head of state and the bishop of Urgel in Spain.

The colours of the Andorran flag are those of France and Spain. Some people have attributed the origin of the present flag to Napoleon III.

There are two versions of the state coat of arms. The quarters of the Spanish version represent the crozier and miter of the bishop of Urgel, the coats of arms of Catalonia and of the counts of Foix, and the coat of arms of the counts of Béarn, with two cows. The French version is topped by a crown of gold, and the two Béarn cows face in the other direction.

State arms

State flag

49

Gibraltar

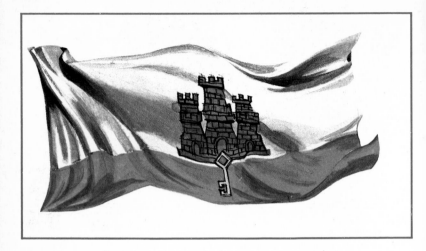

Gibraltar is located on a narrow peninsula on the south coast of Spain and is one of the two· traditional "Pillars of Hercules" which once marked the limits of the world known to Europeans.

A British possession since 1713, Gibraltar is now Great Britain's sole colony in Europe. Since 1969 this crown colony has enjoyed considerable powers of self-government.

Although the colony's official state flag is that of Great Britain, an unofficial civil flag has existed since 1966. This banner is a flag version of the colony's coat of arms.

The castle with three towers and the key symbolize Gibraltar's strategic position in the Mediterranean. The motto *Montis Insignia Calpe* ("The Badge of Mount Calpe") recalls that Gibraltar was formerly known as Calpe.

The present name comes from the Arabic Gebel Tariq (Mount Tariq), from Tariq ibn Ziyad, who conquered the peninsula in AD 711.

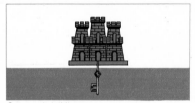

State and civil flag

State arms

Italy

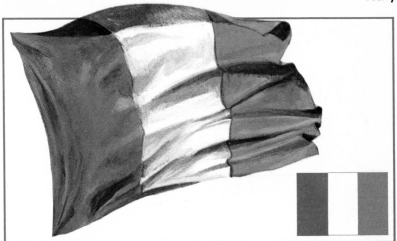

The Italian tricolour comes from the standard designed by Napoleon during the Italian campaign of 1796 and was first adopted, in its simplest form, by the Cisalpine Republic in 1798. Charged with the coat of arms of the House of Savoy, this flag became that of the kingdom of Italy in 1861. When the monarchy came to an end in 1946, the coat of arms was removed and a simple tricolour replaced the older flag. The present flag was officially adopted on June 19, 1946.

Four maritime republics are commemorated in the quarters of the shield of the war and civil ensigns.

State arms

Venice is represented by the winged lion of St. Mark with an open book. Genoa is represented by the red cross of St. George. The Maltese cross represents Amalfi, while the Pisan cross stands for Pisa. The war ensign shows the lion of St. Mark with a sword. Above the shield is a naval crown.

The state arms are enclosed by olive and oak branches, symbolizing peace and strength. The star represents the state, and the cogwheel stands for labour.

War ensign

San Marino

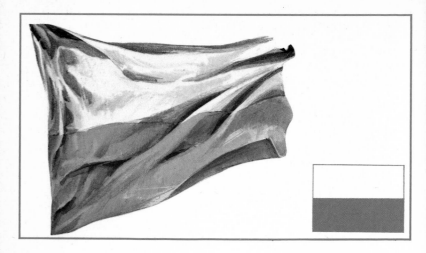

The small Republic of San Marino is located in the Apennines between the Emilia-Romagna and Marche regions of Italy. It is one of the oldest nations of Europe, and its first statutes date from the thirteenth century.

The white and blue of the flag, which were probably adopted in the eighteenth century, symbolize snow and sky.

The state coat of arms is encircled by a wreath of oak and laurel. The white towers topped with ostrich plumes represent the three towers built on the peak of Mount Titano. Another interpretation suggests that the ostrich feathers (*penne* in Italian) stand for the Apennines. The crown symbolizes the sovereignty of the state. The motto *Libertas* recalls the number of fugitives who found refuge in the republic, especially during the Italian wars of independence.

State arms

State and war flag

The ratification of the Lateran Pacts in 1929 marked the end of hostilities between Italy and the Holy See. It was at this time that the yellow and white flag that had been used by the Pontifical States until 1870 was revived. White and yellow had been adopted as the papal colours in 1808 by Pius VII.

The red field of the coat of arms recalls that red was once the colour of the Catholic Church. The keys of St. Peter and the tiara are symbols of the Pope's authority. The keys commemorate the Pope's power of deliberating in the spiritual and temporal realms.

State arms

Coat of arms of Pope John Paul II

53

Malta

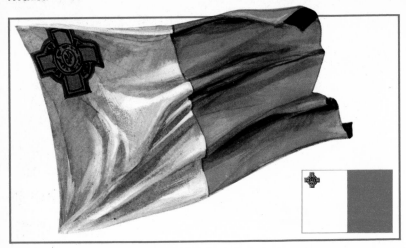

Malta was invaded by the Arabs in the ninth century and conquered by the Normans in 1090. Since then the colours of Count Roger, white and red, have always been associated with the island's history. When Malta became independent in 1964, the white and red flag previously in use was maintained. The George Cross, which is depicted in the flag and in the coat of arms, was awarded to the island by Great Britain in 1943 for courage shown during World War II. The eight-pointed white cross (the Maltese cross) on a red field was adopted for Malta's merchant fleet in 1965. It refers to the long association of Malta with the Knights of St. John of Jerusalem, who settled in the island in 1530 after the Turkish occupation of Cyprus and Rhodes. The coat of arms features a traditional boat, the prickly pear, and tools used by local farmers. The design replaces a shield designed by British heralds.

State arms

Civil ensign

Yugoslavia is now a federal republic, but it was born in 1918 as a monarchy, from the union of the kingdoms of Serbia and Montenegro with the provinces of Bosnia, Herzegovina, Croatia, Slovenia, and Dalmatia.

Blue, white, and red are traditional Slavic colours. These colours were used in the nineteenth century in the flags of Serbia and Montenegro. The federal republic adopted the same flag on January 31, 1946, but replaced the royal coat of arms with the red star of Communism. The same flag is also used by the merchant marine, but the dimensions are

State arms

different (2:3 instead of 1:2).

The six flames in the coat of arms represent the six republics that form the federation. The date November 29, 1943, commemorates the foundation of the National Liberation Committee.

The flags of the individual republics, which were adopted between 1945 and 1946, repeat the national colours, with variations. Only Macedonia has an all-red flag.

Presidential flag

55

Yugoslavia

War ensign

Civil and state ensign

Republics of Yugoslavia

Slovenia

Croatia

Bosnia and Herzegovina

Montenegro

Serbia

Macedonia

Bulgaria

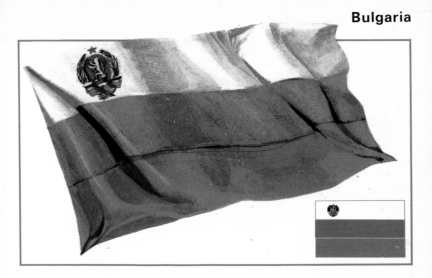

The basic Bulgarian national tricolour was adopted in 1878. The colours white, green and red represent love of peace, products of the earth, and the people's courage, respectively.

The two dates recorded in the coat of arms (adopted in 1971) commemorate the settlement of the Bulgars in their land and the end of the Nazi occupation. The ears of grain and the cogwheel stand for agriculture and industry. The rampant lion was a Bulgarian emblem as early as the fourteenth century. The red star symbolizes Communism.

State arms

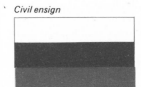

Civil ensign

War ensign

Flag of the chairman of the council of ministers

57

Albania

When Albania became independent in 1912 after centuries of Turkish domination, the red flag with a two-headed eagle was revived. This flag had been used in the fifteenth century by the national hero Skanderbeg in honour of an ancient tradition that the first Albanians were descendants of an eagle.

The modern flag was modified a few times. The current one dates from March 15, 1946. In this the eagle is topped by a red star, the symbol of Communism. The date of the Congress of Permet—May 24, 1944—is commemorated in the national coat of arms.

State arms

War ensign

Civil ensign

58

The Greek liberation movement, which got under way in the late eighteenth century, finally achieved success in 1830 with the recognition of national sovereignty. White and blue were colours adopted during the Greek wars of independence, and this choice was confirmed in 1833 when Otto of Bavaria ascended the throne of Greece. Blue and white were also the colours of his family.

The flag that was most recently officially readopted in 1978 is similar to the one used in 1822, although the blue is a darker shade. This flag is also used by the navy and the merchant fleet. The cross in the canton is a symbol of religious belief. It is generally believed that the nine stripes stand for the nine syllables of the Greek motto *Eleuthería a thánatos* ("Liberty or Death").

State arms

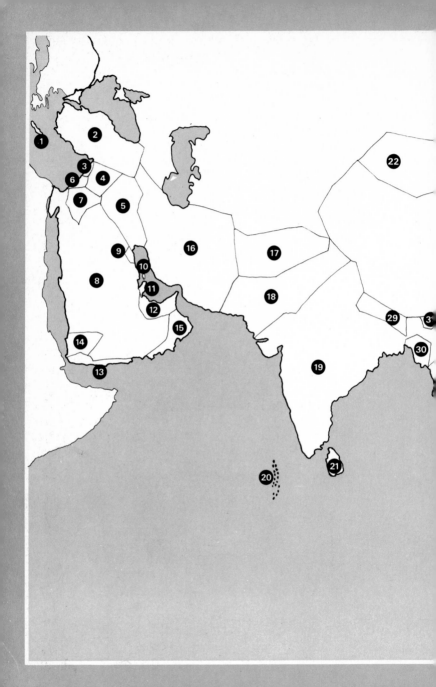

Asia

Cyprus

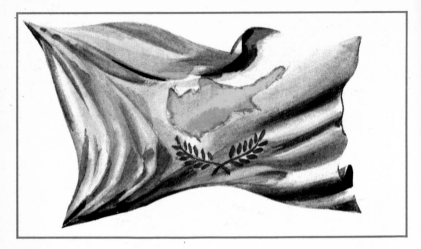

An agreement between Great Britain, Greece, and Turkey brought British sovereignty in Cyprus to an end in 1960.

A map of the island is represented in the flag that was adopted in 1960. It is shown in yellow, referring to the deposits of copper for which Cyprus has been known since ancient times. The two olive branches refer to the spirit of peace and cooperation that was aspired to by the Greek and Turkish populations of the island. The dove with an olive branch represented in the coat of arms repeats the message conveyed in the flag. The year of independence, 1960, is also commemorated in the national emblem.

Incidents between the Greek and Turkish communities, which culminated in the Greek seizure of power in 1974 and the subsequent Turkish invasion of the island, have resulted in the virtual division of the island in two. The Greek and Turkish flags have all but replaced the Cypriot flag in the two areas, and in the military bases controlled by Great Britain the Union Jack is flown.

State arms

State and war flag and ensign

The red in the Turkish flag dates to the time of the Ottomans, who converted the country to Islam in the thirteenth century. The crescent moon and the star go back to the cult of Diana and to the Virgin Mary. About the fifteenth century they became symbolic of Islam, but they were especially associated with Ottoman rule in Turkey.

These symbols were kept when Turkey became a republic in 1923. The present form of the flag was confirmed in 1936. The history of the flag is unclear. Historical sources and local legends and traditions connected with the expansion of the Ottoman Empire often conflict.

Presidential flag

State arms

Lebanon

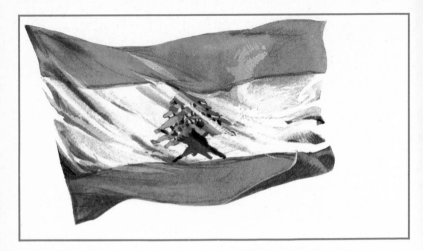

The tree shown in the Lebanese flag is one of the famous cedars of Lebanon mentioned in the Bible, and symbolizes strength, holiness, and eternity. Red stands for self-sacrifice and white stands for peace. The two colours are also related to the Kaisites and Yemenites who controlled the

National flag

State arms

country until the eighteenth century. The present flag was adopted in 1943 when Lebanon became independent. Earlier, when the country was administered by France, the cedar was depicted on the white band of the French Tricolour.

The coat of arms, which is not official, also bears the same emblem as the flag.

Syria became fully independent in 1946 and officially adopted the green, white, and black tricolour with three red stars. This flag had been used unofficially since the 1920s. In 1958 Syria joined Egypt in the United Arab Republic and a new flag was introduced—a red, white, and black tricolour charged with two green stars. When Syria withdrew from the United Arab Republic in 1961, the former flag was revived. Two years later another one was introduced. It was identical with that of the United Arab Republic except for a third star in the central band. In 1971 Syria joined Egypt and Libya in a new union (the Federation of Arab

State arms

Republics), and a red, white, and black tricolour bearing a gold hawk was introduced.

In 1980 Syria again adopted the United Arab Republic flag of 1958–1961.

National flag

Iraq

National flag

The present Iraqi flag was adopted in July 1963, after the Qassim regime was overthrown. The three green stars are derived from a proposed union with Egypt and Syria which never materialized. The country's pan-Arab sympathies, however, are reflected in the traditional colours of the flag. Red stands for courage, white for generosity, black for the conquests of Islam. Green is the traditional colour of Islam.

The coat of arms consists of Saladin's eagle charged with a shield bearing the national colours. The Kufic inscription gives the name of the country.

State arms

The Israeli flag is inspired by the *talith*, the Jewish prayer shawl, and was created by the Zionist movement at the end of the nineteenth century. The flag was offically adopted a few months after the birth of the new state of Israel. The shield of David is shown in the center of the flag.

The coat of arms shows the *menorah*, the seven-branched candlestick of the Temple of Jerusalem. It is framed by olive branches. The Hebrew inscription is the name of the state.

State arms

War ensign

Civil ensign

Jordan

Royal arms

Royal flag

The Emirate of Transjordan was established by Britain after World War I and became the independent kingdom of Jordan in 1946.

A first version of the Jordanian flag was used by King Hussein of Hejaz. This version was introduced in 1917. The present version was devised by his son, Abdullah, who changed the order of the colours. He added a seven-pointed star on a red field in honour of the first seven verses of the Koran.

Saladin's eagle, an extremely popular emblem in the Arab world, is shown in the coat of arms. The eagle is shown on a blue globe and represents the spread of Islam throughout the world. The ears of grain and the palm leaves represent typical products of Jordan. The inscription on the scroll can be translated "Al-Hussein Ibn Talal Ibn Abdullah, King of the Hashemite Kingdom of Jordan, prays that God may grant him happiness and help."

The stern orthodoxy of the Wahabis, who came to power in the early twentieth century with Ibn Saud, is reflected in the traditional Islamic green of the flag and in the inscription on both sides of it: "There is no God but Allah; Muhammad Is the Prophet of Allah."

The crossed swords in the coat of arms represent the will to defend the faith. The date palm refers to agriculture and is the symbol of the oasis in the desert.

State arms

Royal flag

Kuwait

The state of Kuwait, formerly a British protectorate, became fully independent in 1961. The same year the new state adopted a flag whose colours reflect the country's membership of the Arab world.

Green stands for the earth, white for the country's achievements, red for the shed blood of enemies, and black for the battlefields.

Kuwait is on the Persian Gulf and, like the United Arab Emirates, has a falcon in its coat of arms, together with a *dhow*, the typical local ship. The name of the state is shown in the inscription.

Ensign; state flag

State arms

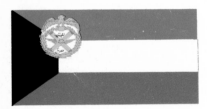

War flag

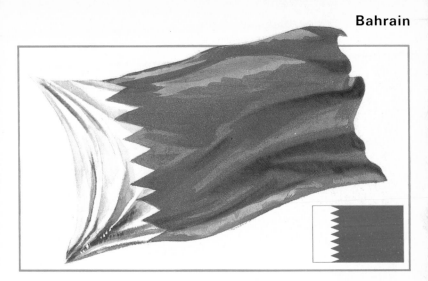

This archipelago in the Persian Gulf was formerly a British protectorate. It obtained full independence in 1971 and is ruled by a hereditary monarchy.

The present flag, which was adopted in 1933, is red with a white band in the hoist. The two areas are sometimes divided by serration, sometimes by a straight line. The choice of a bicolour goes back to an Anglo-Arab agreement in the nineteenth century. At the time the states of the Persian Gulf were required to use a red flag with a white border. Red was the colour of the Kharijite Muslims.

The state coat of arms was designed by Sir Charles Belgrave, the sheikh's political adviser. It was originally topped by a crown, the symbol of royal authority, but this was subsequently abolished.

The sheikh's personal standard has two white bands, one along the top and the other along the bottom.

State arms

Royal flag

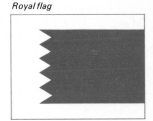

Qatar

The emirate of Qatar, located on a peninsula in the Persian Gulf, was formerly a British protectorate. It has been fully independent since 1971. Qatar's original flag, like those of neighbouring states, was red. The white band in the hoist was added in the middle of the nineteenth century. The serration between the red and the white has no special meaning. The change from red to maroon is due to the effect of sunlight on the red dye used in making the flags. This colour was introduced about 1949.

The coat of arms includes the name of the state, a *dhow*, two scimitars, and two palm branches.

State arms

National flag

The seven independent sheikhdoms that formerly comprised Trucial Oman, or the Trucial States, formed a new nation in 1971. These seven states—Abu Dhabi, Dubai, Sharjah, Ajman, Umm al Qaiwain, Ras al Khaimah, and Fujairah—were formerly protectorates of Great Britain. The chief resource of the United Arab Emirates on the coast of the Persian Gulf is oil.

The white and red of the flag appeared in the flags of the individual sheikhdoms from the beginning of the nineteenth century, when the use of these colours was imposed by Great Britain.

The present national flag was adopted late in 1971. In addition to red and white, the colours green and black are those of the pan-Arab movement, which is supported by the new state. The falcon is the main element in the coat of arms. The ship is the traditional *dhow* used by the Arabs in the gulf. The name of the state is shown at the base of the coat of arms.

National flag

State arms

Flags of the emirates

Fujairah

Dubai

Ras al Khaimah

Abu Dhabi

Ajman

Umm al Qaiwain

74

People's Democratic Republic of Yemen

This republic, also known as South Yemen, has been independent since 1967. It was constituted by the union of the British-controlled territories called the South Arabian Federation and the Aden Protectorates. The flag, which was adopted at the end of 1967, is basically that of the National Liberation Front, the pan-Arab red, white, and black tricolour. The blue triangle stands for the people, the star for the National Liberation Front. The red stripe in the flag denotes the revolution, the white peace, and the black the country's colonial past.

The coat of arms consists of Saladin's eagle, a shield with the national colours, and the name of the state.

State arms

National flag

75

Yemen Arab Republic

The present flag was adopted in 1962 after the revolution that overthrew the monarchy. This flag shows the new state's support of the cause of Arab unity and differs from the Syrian flag only in the use of a single star, symbol of independence. Red stands for the revolution, white for purity and faith in the future, and black for the country's past.

The eagle in the national emblem symbolizes the strength and tenacity of the Yemeni people. Also shown in the national emblem are a coffee plant and the old Marib dam. (Coffee

National flag

has become less important in the local economy.) The name of the state is shown in the scroll.

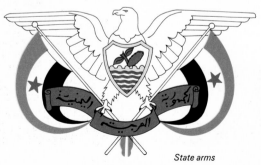

State arms

Oman

This independent sultanate on the eastern coast of the Arabian peninsula was called Muscat and Oman until 1970. The sultanate's ties with Great Britain date to the early nineteenth century.

Kharÿite Muslims, who account for most of the population, have used red flags in the area of the Persian Gulf for centuries. This tradition is maintained in the new flag adopted in 1970. The state arms, which are also included in the national flag, consist of two crossed swords and the *gambia*, the typical local knife.

State arms

National flag

War ensign

77

Iran

Following the revolution of 1906, the traditional colours of Iran (green, white, and red) were adopted for the national flag in the form of horizontal stripes. Special flags for the government and military services included the national emblem (a rising sun and a lion holding a sword) on the central stripe.

The revolution of 1979 substituted the new national coat of arms (in red instead of green) as the central emblem. The arms are in the form of a globe to indicate the worldwide struggle of oppressed peoples. The four crescents and sword symbolize the Islamic faith and strength. The mark at the top above the sword stands for fortitude. All the elements of the arms taken together constitute a stylized graphic rendition of the word Allah (God), indicating the importance of religion to the country. The five main elements of the arms correspond to the five religious obligations of Muslims.

Along the top of the red stripe and the

State arms

bottom of the green stripe of the flag appears the inscription "God Is Great." It is repeated twenty-two times to recall the twenty-second of the month of Bahman (February 11, 1979), when the revolution which led to the Islamic Republic of Iran succeeded. The traditional interpretations of the flag colours are the Islamic faith (green), peace (white), and valour (red).

Afghanistan

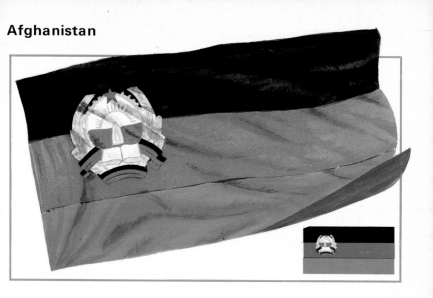

In 1929, following his European tour, King Amanullah introduced a vertical tricolour as the national flag of Afghanistan. Black stood for the past, red for the blood shed for independence, and green for hope in the future. Although the exact form of the flag has been changed several times, these colours are now recognized as the national colours.

On April 21, 1980, the present designs of the flag and coat of arms were officially established. Black recalls flags used by Afghanistan in the past; red is for the blood of heroes; and green is a symbol of the Islamic faith, prosperity, and victory over imperialism.

In the coat of arms the national colours are repeated as a ribbon holding a wreath of wheat—a reminder of the agricultural basis of the nation. At the top is a cogwheel (for industrialization) and a star symbolic of luck, victory, and Communism.

The liberation of the people and the dawn of a new day are suggested by the rising sun, while the open book at the bottom of the arms is seen as an emblem of enlightenment and of the scientific and cultural enrichment being brought to the people.

The center of the coat of arms has a stylized rendition of the Muslim pulpit. There are two parts to this— the *mihrab* (an alcove in the wall of a mosque indicating the direction of Mecca) and the *minbar*, or pulpit proper.

State arms

79

Pakistan

The crescent and star on a green field were adopted in 1906 by the All-India Muslim League. The same motif was adopted by Pakistan when it became an independent state in 1947. The white stripe towards the staff stands for the country's religious minorities. A more recent interpretation sees white as the colour of peace and green as that of prosperity. The national flag, with different proportions, is also used by the navy.

The shield of the coat of arms is framed by a narcissus wreath. Within the shield are the chief agricultural products of the country. The motto is "Faith, Unity, Discipline."

State arms

Civil ensign

Presidential flag

The Indian flag was developed during the first two decades of the twentieth century. Originally, a spinning wheel was shown in the white band. With this symbol Gandhi tried to point up the need for self-sufficiency. The version of the flag that was officially adopted in 1947 has the *chakra* in place of the spinning wheel. This is an ancient Indian symbol associated with the powers and changes of nature. The colour blue refers to sky and sea, and the twenty-four spokes stand for the hours of the day. Originally, orange stood for the Hindu population, green for the Muslims. White symbolizes the spirit of conciliation between the two populations. Officially orange is the symbol of courage, white peace and truth, and green faith. The *chakra's* function of harmonizing natural occurrences is underlined in another interpretation of the colours. Here orange and green stand for the natural resources, and white for the preservation of life.

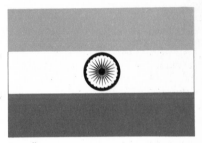

State flag

The *chakra* is also depicted in the national arms, along with a capital of one of the columns in the holy city of Sarnath from the time of Emperor Asoka (third century B.C.). The quotation from the *Upanishads* can be translated as "Only Virtue Triumphs." St. George's cross in the war ensign reflects India's connection with Great Britain and other Commonwealth countries. Private citizens may display the civil ensign on their boats.

India

War flag

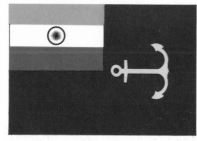

State ensign

State arms

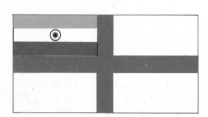

War ensign

Civil ensign

Maldives

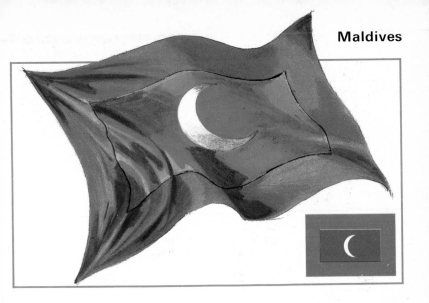

The present flag of the Maldives was adopted in 1965. The crescent and the green field are traditional Islamic symbols. Red was the colour of the flag used by several other countries on the Indian Ocean. A more recent interpretation sees the red and the green as symbols of the blood that was shed to achieve freedom and of the hope for peace.

The national emblem shows two national flags, a date palm, and the star and crescent of Islam. The inscription is the name of the state.

State arms

Prime minister's flag

War flag

Sri Lanka

The present flag dates from 1978, the year that Ceylon became the Democratic Socialist Republic of Sri Lanka. The basic Sinhalese flag was raised in 1948, when the country (then known as Ceylon) gained independence. It was modified in 1951, when green and orange stripes were added to represent the Hindu and Muslim minorities. The lion with a sword dates to the sixth century B.C. The four *pipul* leaves are Buddhist symbols.

The lotus and the wheel, which are also Buddhist symbols, are shown in the coat of arms. The rice represents abundance, while the sun and moon symbolize the hope of long life for the country. These symbols also appear in the flag of Nepal.

State arms

Presidential flag

War flag

Mongolia

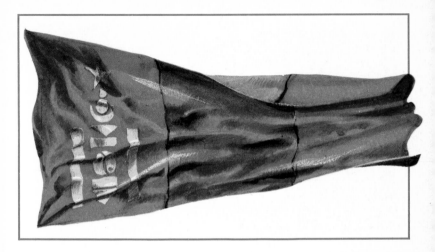

The flag was first adopted in 1945 and confirmed in 1949. The five-pointed star on the red ground stands for Communism. Blue, representing the sky, is the national colour. Yellow is considered the colour of brotherhood. The *soyonbo* ideogram is one of the oldest symbols of Mongolia and is rich in mystical connotations. The elements that comprise this symbol are fire, earth, water, the sun, the moon, and *yin* and *yang*. *Yin* and *yang* are also depicted in the flag of Korea. The placement of the star and *soyonbo* stands for the harmony between the traditions of Mongolia and the international ideals of the state.

The horseman riding towards the sun in the state arms stands for the country's faith in its Communist future. Agriculture and industry are symbolized by ears of grain and the cogwheel. The star and the *soyonbo*, together with the Cyrillic initials of the name of the state, are depicted in the arms.

National flag

State arms

85

People's Republic of China

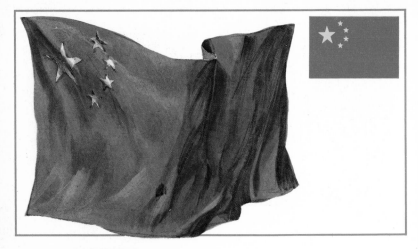

State arms

War flag

The five-pointed star in the Chinese flag is for Communism, but the number five also stood for wholeness and perfection in Chinese philosophy. The four smaller stars represent the four classes of workers, agricultural, industrial, white collar, and managerial. Although red is the colour of Communism, it is also one of the five colours of old Chinese flags. The other four were blue, white, black, and yellow.

The coat of arms is framed by ears of rice and wheat, while industrial activity is represented by the cogwheel. The Gate of Heavenly Peace, the entryway to the former Forbidden City of Peking, is also shown. This symbolizes the return of power to that city.

The ideograms (8, 1) on the war flag commemorate August 1, 1928, the date of the formation of the People's Liberation Army.

State and war ensign

Governor's flag

This British crown colony consists of the island of Hong Kong, the territory of Kowloon, and the island of Lantau.

The flag is the British ensign charged with the coat of arms of the colony. The Union Jack is also flown.

The coat of arms contains two three-masted junks and a naval crown. The shield is supported by a lion, symbolizing Great Britain, and by a dragon, symbolizing China.

State arms

Republic of China (Taiwan)

The Nationalist Chinese flag dates from 1914. Its design corresponds to the political principles of Sun Yat-sen, the founder and first president of the Republic of China.

The sun, which also appears in the state arms, was the Kuomintang party symbol. Red stands for the sacrifice of the people and also for the largest ethnic group, the Hans. White symbolizes frankness and brotherhood, blue, equality and justice.

State arms

Presidential flag

War flag

Civil ensign

The (North) Korean flag, adopted in 1948, combines the new and the old. White is traditionally the colour of purity, while blue stands for the hope of peace. The red band and the five-pointed star stand for Communism. The white disk charged with a star may relate to the *yin* and *yang* symbol (*t'aeguk* in Korean), which in Chinese philosophy expresses the opposing principles of nature (day and night, water and fire, etc.).

National flag

Sheaves of rice surround the national coat of arms. The main theme of the emblem is the industrialization of the country. A hydroelectric plant is shown against a mountain landscape. The red star stands for Communism. The name of the country is inscribed in the scroll.

State arms

Republic of Korea

State arms

This flag was first raised officially in the late nineteenth century. It was then used throughout the country north and south. The flag was revived in 1948 and modified, and was officially adopted by (South) Korea in 1950.

The white field stands for peace and purity. The *yin* and *yang* symbol is shown in the center. In the work of the Chinese philosopher Chu-Hsi, *yin* and *yang* represented the opposing forces of nature, including sky and earth, male and female, summer and winter. Similar meaning is attributed to the four trigrams (*kwae*), which may represent the seasons, the four cardinal points of the compass, etc.

In the national coat of arms the *yin* and *yang* are framed by rose of Sharon petals. This flower grows throughout Korea and is considered a symbol of strength and tenacity.

War ensign and jack

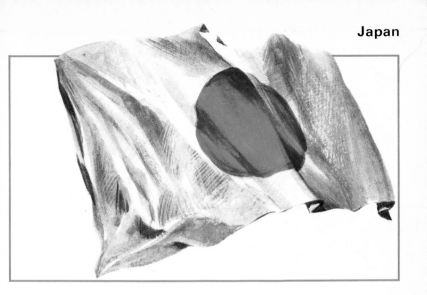

For more than a thousand years, the sun has been the fundamental element in Japanese flags. The sun is the legendary ancestor of the emperor, and it is the symbol of the land of the rising sun. The national flag (*Hi-no-maru*, "Sun Disk") consists of a red sun on a white field. This was originally the flag of the Tokugawa and was adopted by the state in 1870. The war flag and war ensign are variations on the sun symbol.

The emperor's *mon* (emblem) consists of a stylized chrysanthemum with sixteen petals. The *mon* appears on a red field in the imperial standard. The flags of the prefectures are remarkable for their elegance of design and for their often unusual colours.

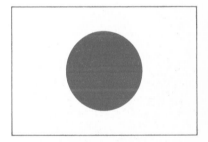

Civil and state flag and ensign

Imperial arms

Japan

Imperial flag

Prime minister's flag

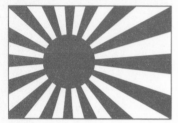

War ensign

War flag

Prefectures of Japan

Hokkaido

Aomori

Akita

Iwate

Yamagata

Miyagi

Niigata

Toyama

Ishikawa

Fukushima

Nagano

Gumma

Prefectures of Japan

Tochigi

Ibaraki

Fukui

Gifu

Kanagawa

Saitama

Tokyo

Yamanashi

Chiba

Shiga

Aichi

Shizuoka

Shimane

Tottori

Hyogo

Osaka

Prefectures of Japan

Mie

Yamaguchi

Hiroshima

Okayama

Nara

Tokushima

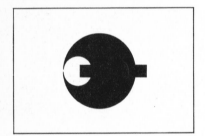

Wakayama

Ehime

Kōchi

Fukuoka

Saga

Kumamoto

Oita

Miyazaki

Kagoshima

Okinawa

Nepal

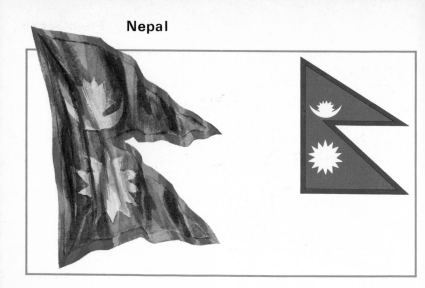

Nepal is the only nation in the world that has no national flag not rectangular in shape. It was adopted in 1962. The sun and moon are symbolic of the hope that the country may live as long as the two astral bodies.

The Nepalese landscape, with the Himalayas in the background, is the chief feature of the national coat of arms. Local fauna and flora are represented by a white cow, a pheasant, and rhododendrons. The two Gurkhas, one in British uniform, commemorate the military valour of the Nepalese. Also shown in the emblem are crossed swords, the sun and moon, two national flags, Buddha's footprints, and the royal crown. The motto inscribed below can be translated "The Fatherland Is More Important Than the Kingdom of Heaven."

State arms

Royal arms

Royal flag

Bangladesh

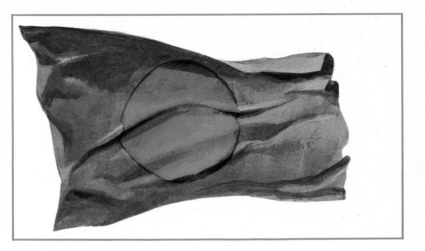

Bangladesh was proclaimed an independent republic on March 26, 1971, after having separated from Pakistan. Before then it was the eastern province of Pakistan, separated from West Pakistan by India.

The green field of the flag refers to agriculture and to the country's connection with the Islamic world. The majority of the people are Muslim. The red disk symbolizes the blood shed to achieve independence. The disk is somewhat closer to the staff than to the fly so that it will appear in the center when the flag is rippling in the wind.

In the national emblem some of the chief products of the country are depicted, including a stylized water lily, jute leaves, and *padi* (rice) stalks. The waters shown are the Ganges and the Brahmaputra. The four stars refer to the political aims of the revolution.

State arms

National flag on land

Bhutan

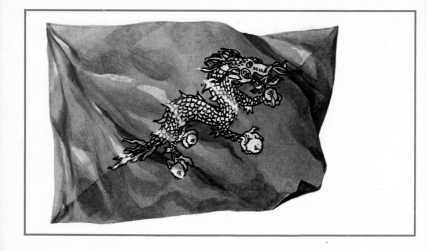

National flag

Royal arms

Bhutan was formerly subject to China and Great Britain but the country signed a treaty in 1949 entrusting national defense and foreign policy to India.

Bhutan's former links with China left traces in the national flag, which has been in use since the nineteenth century. The flag is divided diagonally. The upper half is saffron yellow, the colour of royal authority. The lower half is reddish orange, representing Buddhism. The dragon is a benevolent figure in the Orient and is associated with power and generosity. It has particular significance for Bhutan, for the Tibetan name of the country, Druk-Yul, can be translated either "Land of the Dragon" or "Land of Thunder." Popular tradition associates the thunder of the mountain valleys with the voice of the dragon.

In the national arms, the thunderbolts between the two dragons symbolize the authority of the Buddhist monks.

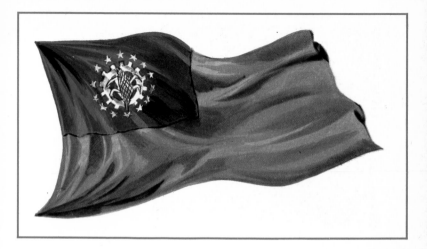

During World War II, the Burmese resistance movement adopted a red flag with a white star next to the staff. When the country obtained full independence from Great Britain in 1948, a similar flag was adopted. The resistance star appeared on a blue field and five smaller stars represented the five ethnic components of the country. Red stands for courage, and blue stands for the night sky with stars, a symbol of progress and purity. The flag was modified after the socialist constitution of 1974. The cogwheel and rice were added on the blue field to represent workers and peasants, and the fourteen stars stand for the states into which the country is divided.

In the center of the national arms, over the cogwheel, is a map of the country. The two lions at the sides, a recurrent theme in Burmese iconography, stand for strength tempered by wisdom. The name of the country appears in the scroll.

State arms

National flag

101

Thailand

Royal arms

The white elephant, symbol of the kings of Thailand, used to be the main element in the national flag. It now appears only in the war ensign. The present flag was adopted in 1917. The red and white stripes stand for the sacrifice and purity of the Thai people. Blue is the royal colour of Thailand.

The Garuda, which appears in the royal arms, is the mythical bird on which Vishnu rode.

War flag

War ensign

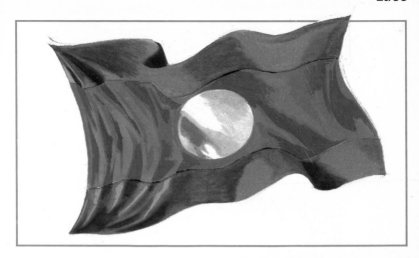

Throughout much of Laos's history, the country has been subject to foreign influence. In the eighteenth century Laos was caught up in the wars between Vietnam, Burma, and Siam. It was subsequently occupied by the Siamese and then by the French. Early in the twentieth century, the French linked Laos with their other Indochinese possessions. Laos has been independent since 1952, but it has been the theater of violent conflict between nationalist, pro-Communist (Pathet Lao), and neutralist forces. The Pathet Lao reached agreement with the government in Vientiane, the capital, in 1973 and came into power. In 1975 Laos was transformed from a monarchy into a people's democratic republic.

The new flag is the one that was used for years by the Pathet Lao. The former national flag showed three elephants and a parasol, representing the three divisions of the country and the authority of the sovereign.

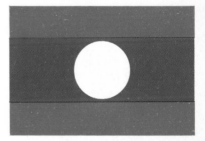

National flag

State arms

People's Republic of Kampuchea and Democratic Kampuchea

State arms of the People's Republic

National flag of the People's Republic

In the mid-nineteenth century, France took control of the small but ancient Southeast Asian country known to its inhabitants as Kampuchea. The French name for the country was Cambodge, anglicized as Cambodia. In 1975 the traditional name was reestablished.

The present national flag is the fifth official banner of the country since 1945. All the flags, however, have had in common the use of the symbol of a temple, Kampuchea's greatest national monument, Angkor Wat, a magnificent thirteenth-century city.

The colour red has also appeared in all the flags flown by Kampuchea of which we have record, but it has recently taken on a new meaning. In 1970 the neutralist kingdom of Cambodia was overthrown and a pro-Western government under the name of the Khmer Republic established. The former had used a flag of blue-red-blue horizontal stripes with a white representation of Angkor Wat

National flag of Democratic Kampuchea

State arms of Democratic Kampuchea

in the center. The Khmer Republic took the white-temple-on-red emblem as a canton for its blue flag, adding three white stars.

On April 17, 1975, Communist forces known as the Khmer Rouge established a new regime in which red was recognized as a colour of revolution and Communism. The following year a new constitution was promulgated for the country, which was renamed Democratic Kampuchea. The constitution described the new flag as a red field with a three-towered "national monument" (i.e., Angkor Wat) in the center. A new coat of arms was also introduced at that time to reflect the ideological orientation of the regime. It shows fields of rice separated by an irrigation canal and, in the distance, a factory. Sheaves of rice, bound with the red ribbon on which the name of the country appears, complete the design.

In January 1979 Democratic Kampuchea was conquered by another group of Cambodian Communists, backed by the army of Vietnam. The People's Republic of Kampuchea was proclaimed and a new national flag officially hoisted. It differs from the flag of Democratic Kampuchea only in having a temple of five towers instead of three in the center. The same temple is represented on a red disk in the coat of arms of the People's Republic. Below is a cogwheel symbolizing industry; sheaves of rice for agriculture frame the design. Again, a red ribbon bearing the name of the country in gold is wrapped around the rice.

International political alignments have allowed the government of Democratic Kampuchea to maintain its diplomatic relations and its recognition by the United Nations as the official government of Kampuchea. Khmer Rouge soldiers still operate in the western part of the country, the rest of which is effectively controlled by the Vietnamese army and the government of the People's Republic. Thus at the time this is written, both national flags and coats of arms are in actual use and are recognized by various foreign governments.

Vietnam

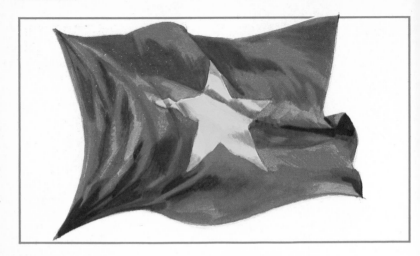

The proclamation of the Socialist Republic of Vietnam on July 2, 1976, brought an end to one of the longest conflicts in modern history and to a division of the country that had lasted thirty years.

The national flag and the national arms, which were both adopted when the new state was constituted, had been used by North Vietnam, the flag since 1955, and the emblem since 1956. Red stands for the revolution and for the blood shed by the Vietnamese people. The five-pointed yellow star stands for the unity of workers, peasants, intellectuals, youths, and soldiers.

The garland of rice, the country's main agricultural product, and the cogwheel represent agriculture and industry.

State arms

National flag

106

The Philippine flag was first used by General Emilio Aguinaldo, leader of the liberation struggle, in 1898. It had been adopted by the leaders of the independence movement in exile in Hong Kong.

The white triangle at the staff stands for the liberation movement against Spain. The stars stand for the main regions of the country: Luzon, Mindanao, and the Visayan archipelago. The eight rays of the sun stand for the first eight provinces to revolt against Spain. The blue and red refer to magnanimity and courage. (These two colours are reversed in wartime.) White stands for peace.

The lion in the coat of arms goes back to the period of Spanish domination, while the eagle dates from the time when the country was subject to American rule. The sun in the center represents the country's independence.

State arms

Malaysia

In 1963 the eleven Malay states joined with Sabah and Sarawak (territories of former British Borneo) and with Singapore to form the Federation of Malaysia. The flag adopted that year had fourteen stripes and a fourteen-pointed star, representing the fourteen states of the federation. The flag remained unchanged when Singapore left the federation in 1965.

White and red have long been traditional colours throughout Southeast Asia. The blue in the flag is connected with the Union Jack and Malaysia's links with the British Commonwealth. The royal colour yellow stands for the nine sultanates of the

National flag on land

Standard of the head of state

State arms

108

War ensign

Civil ensign

federation, while the crescent and star are symbols of Islam.

The coat of arms of the federation shows a shield supported by two tigers. The five Malay *krises* stand for Johore, Kedah, Perlis, Kelantan, and Trengganu. The four quarters in the center represent Selangor, Pahang, Perak, and Negri Sembilan, which appear between the coats of arms of Penang and Malacca. The coats of arms of Sabah and Sarawak below are separated by the hibiscus, the national flower of Malaysia. The hibiscus was added to the coat of arms in 1967 to replace the symbol of Singapore. The motto on the scroll is "Unity Is Strength."

States of Malaysia

Kedah

Perlis

Penang

States of Malaysia

Kelantan

Trengganu

Perak

Pahang

Selangor

Negri Sembilan

Malacca

Johore

Sarawak

Sabah

The state flag of Singapore was adopted in 1959. Red stands for universal brotherhood and white for purity. The crescent and the stars represent a new nation with ideals (symbolized by the stars) of democracy, peace, progress, justice, and equality.

The lion in the coat of arms represents Singapore, "the city of lions." The tiger reflects Singapore's former association with Malaysia. The motto in the coat of arms is "Forward, Singapore."

State arms

War ensign

Civil ensign

Brunei

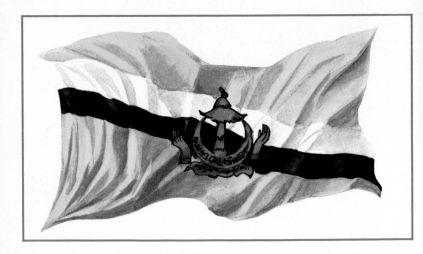

State arms

The sultanate of Brunei, in the northern part of Borneo, has been a British protectorate since 1906. In 1963 the sultanate declined an invitation to join the Federation of Malaysia, preferring to maintain its connection with Great Britain.

The original version of the national flag was adopted in 1906. The national arms were added in 1959. A vertical winged support stands on a crescent, the symbol of the Muslim religion. The Arabic inscriptions read: "Under God's Guidance the Good Shall Prosper," and "Brunei, City of Peace."

Civil ensign; state flag and ensign

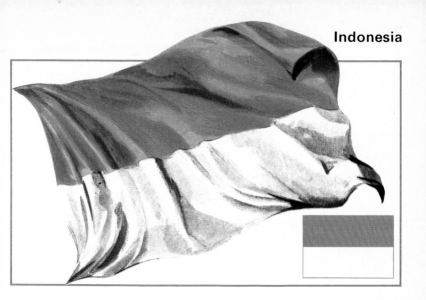

The white and red of Indonesia's flag go back to the late thirteenth century. The national liberation movement revived these colours in 1922. The flag was adopted officially in 1945 when Indonesia became independent. Except for its proportions, the flag is identical with that of Monaco. The sacred bird of Hinduism, the Garuda, is the main element of the coat of arms. The five-pointed star symbolizes religious faith.

The buffalo head stands for the sovereignty of the people and their struggle for independence. The banyan tree symbolizes the national conscience. The branches of *padi* and cotton, providing food and clothing, stand for the nation's prosperity. The chain reflects the equality of the various races that inhabit the nation. The motto is "Unity in Diversity."

State arms

Presidential flag

Africa

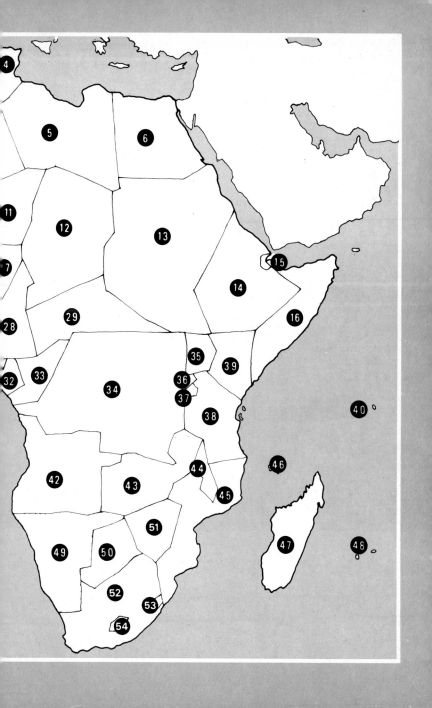

Morocco

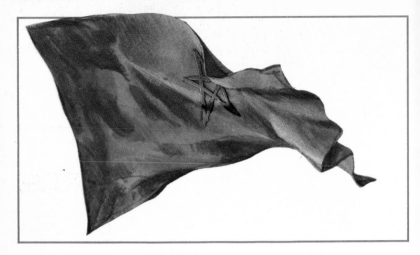

When the kingdom of Morocco became independent in 1956, the flag that had been introduced in 1915 was officially confirmed. Red flags with various emblems had been used for at least three centuries. The green pentacle (or seal of Solomon) was introduced in 1915. From 1912 to 1956 there was a French Tricolour in the canton of the civil ensign.

In the center of the royal coat of arms, the seal of Solomon is shown against the Atlas Mountains. The inscription comes from the Koran and can be translated "If You Help God, He Will Help You."

Royal arms

National flag

War ensign

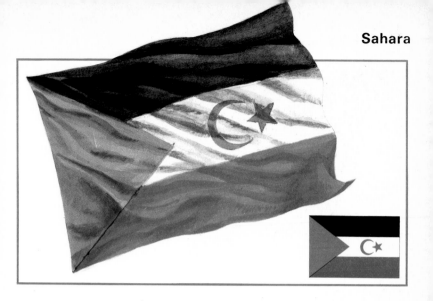

When European imperialist powers divided up Africa, Spain obtained a stretch of northwestern coastland with some hinterland extending into the Sahara Desert. It was ruled as two provinces, Rio de Oro and Saguia el Hamra. One of the last areas in Africa to be freed from colonial rule, Western Sahara—as it came to be known—was abandoned by Spain in 1976 without formal arrangements having been made for independence. Morocco to the north and Mauritania to the south both claimed the territory and agreed to divide it. Nevertheless, many of the local inhabitants wanted an independent state.

The day following the Spanish withdrawal, February 27, 1976, the announcement was made of the Sahraoui Arab Democratic Republic. The Popular Front for the Liberation of Saguia el Hamra and Rio de Oro—known by its acronym POLISARIO—was the organizing force behind the new Sahara state. Military operations were begun and much of the territory has been under POLISARIO control since that time. Militarily exhausted, Mauritania eventually withdrew from the territory it had claimed. This was promptly annexed by Morocco, which is fortifying the coastal areas and phosphate deposits which it controls.

Sahara is recognized as an independent state by many African countries. Its flag combines the four colours common to Arab states throughout Africa and the Near East. Black is for the defeat of enemies, red for the blood on Arab swords, green for fertile lands, and white for purity. The star and crescent are Muslim symbols especially common in North Africa. The same flag design without the star and crescent is recognized as the national flag of Palestine by the Palestine Liberation Organization and others seeking to create an independent Arab state in that territory.

Algeria

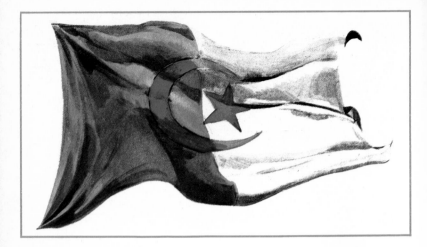

When Algeria became independent on July 3, 1962, it officially adopted the flag that the National Liberation Front had used since 1948. There are conflicting accounts of the origin of this flag. It is traditionally attributed to Abd-el-Kader, the hero of Algerian resistance against the French in the first half of the nineteenth century. But it is more likely that Messali Hadj designed the flag in 1928, after setting up the North African Star political movement.

National flag

White stands for purity. The colour green, the crescent, and the five-pointed star are common symbols in the Islamic world. The star and crescent, originally connected with attributes of the Virgin Mary and Diana, also symbolize Constantinople, the former capital of the Ottoman Empire. The Arabic letters in the seldom-used coat of arms stand for the initials of the name "Algerian Republic."

State arms

The Tunisian flag, in use since the first half of the nineteenth century, is very similar to that of Turkey, which dominated Tunisia from the sixteenth to the nineteenth century.

The red field, the star and crescent were symbols of the Ottoman Empire, common throughout the Islamic world. They were also used by Tunisia from 1881 to 1956, when Tunisia was a French protectorate. The ship shown in the national coat of arms refers to the Phoenician seamen who first landed on the territory of what is now Tunisia. The motto in the shield can be translated "Order, Liberty, and Justice."

State arms

Presidential flag

Libya

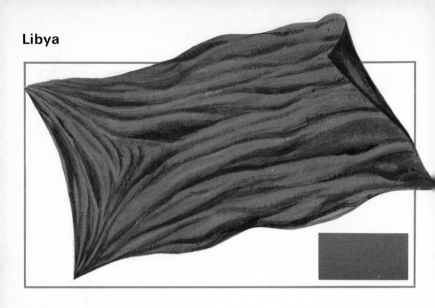

In 1969 the revolutionary leader Colonel Muammar Qaddafi instituted a new national flag. He chose a flag (horizontal red-white-black stripes) similar to the Egyptian flag. In 1971 Libya, Egypt, and Syria formed the Federation of Arab Republics. All three countries flew the same flag, which they hoped would become the basis for the banner of a unified Arab state. This had stripes of the same colours and a coat of arms in the center.

State arms

In 1977 the late President Anwar Sadat of Egypt travelled to Israel to make plans for a peace treaty. Qaddafi felt that the Arab cause had been betrayed and angrily rejected the flag previously in use. As a substitute, Libya hoisted a plain green flag as its national banner; this is a symbol of the "Green Revolution" which Qaddafi has proclaimed. Like many African countries, Libya is struggling to produce enough food for its growing population. Green is also a symbol of the national religion, Islam. The coat of arms of Libya features the name of the country in Arabic script, a shield of the national flag colour, and a hawk. This bird was the totem of the Quraish tribe to which the Prophet Muhammad belonged. The basic design of the coat of arms is similar to the one used by Libya when it was part of the Federation of Arab Republics.

Egypt's importance in the political life of the Islamic countries as a leader in the cause of Arab unity is reflected in the fact that the Egyptian colours appear in the flags of several Near Eastern nations. The present Egyptian colours date to the period immediately following the fall of the monarchy (1952). Red stands for the revolution and the sacrifices of the people, white for the country's bright future, and black for the years in which the country was oppressed. A tricolour with two green stars, the symbol of Egypt's union with Syria in the United Arab Republic, was used from 1958 to 1971. The present flag dates from 1972, when Libya and Syria (which had the same flag) joined Egypt to form the Federation of Arab Republics.

The coat of arms consists of a falcon, the symbol of the Quraish tribe, which was associated with Muhammad.

State arms

War flag

War ensign

Mauritania

State seal

National flag

Mauritania is an Islamic republic in northwestern Africa and is a natural meeting point for the Arab culture of the north and the black culture of the south.

Mauritania has been independent since 1960, but the flag dates from 1959. The green field, the five-pointed star, and the crescent are typical Muslim symbols. Yellow and green, together with red, are common colours in African flags as well. Green is considered the colour of hope and well-being.

The Islamic symbols of star and crescent appear in the state seal (Mauritania has no coat of arms), together with a palm tree and two stalks of millet. The seal was adopted in 1960. The inscriptions in Arabic and French are the name of the state.

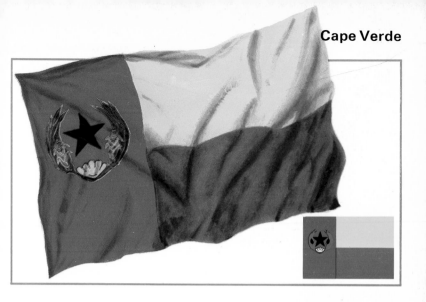

Portuguese explorers reached the Cape Verde Islands in the late fifteenth century when they began their explorations of Africa. Following centuries of colonial rule, the Cape Verde Islands became an independent republic on July 5, 1975. The new national flag was officially hoisted on that day for the first time.

The basic design closely resembles the flag flown by the neighbouring Republic of Guinea-Bissau. Many people working in the liberation movement of these countries hoped that they would eventually unify into a single state, and the similarity of their national flags is a reflection of that desire. The red, yellow, and green colours are those used by other black African nations. They stand for the blood of national heroes in the liberation movement, the hope implicit in the green land of the islands, and the well-being of the people and the harvesting of the fruits of their labour.

State arms

The coat of arms and flag represent by a seashell and ears of corn the fishing and farming which are the livelihood of the people. The black star stands for the independence of an African state. The coat of arms also includes a cogwheel and pick for labour; an open book for culture; and the national motto (in Portuguese)— "Unity, Labour, Progress."

Mali

National flag

State arms

Mali has been independent since September 22, 1960. It is named for one of the great empires of its medieval history. The vertical tricolour was officially adopted on March 1, 1961, and is clearly derived from the French flag. But the colours—green, yellow, and red—are those of several countries of what used to be French Africa. It is more than coincidence that these colours were those of the political movement that led to the state's independence.

Formerly there was a stylized human figure in the middle of the yellow band. This is a very common symbol among the Dogon people of the country. The figure was removed because of demands by the Muslim population who are in the majority: their religion forbids depictions of human beings.

Upper Volta

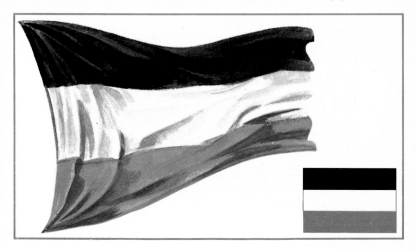

The thousand-mile Volta River of West Africa rises in Upper Volta. There are three branches of this river, the White Volta, the Red Volta, and the Black Volta. Not only is the country named for the river, but the national colours are also derived from the names of its branches. The present flag was adopted in 1959.

The initials of the official name of the country (République de Haute-Volta) are superimposed on the national colours in the coat of arms. The sorghum plant, with two hoes, reflects the importance of this product in the national economy. The motto reads: "Unity, Labour, and Justice."

State arms

Presidential flag

125

Niger

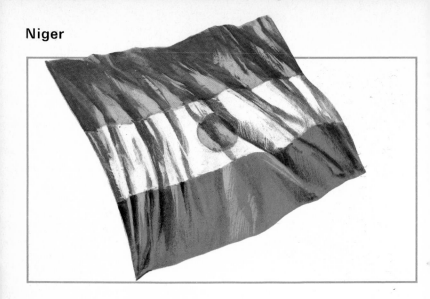

Niger, formerly a French colony, achieved full independence in 1960. The nation adopted a horizontal tricolour the same year. The orange stands for the desert regions of the Sahara, white for purity, and green for hope and the fertile southern territories. The disk in the center is a symbol of the sun.

The state coat of arms was adopted in 1962. In addition to the sun symbol, there are millet leaves and a buffalo head, representing agriculture and animal husbandry, respectively. Past empires that once reigned in the territory are commemorated by the lance and the crossed Tuareg swords.

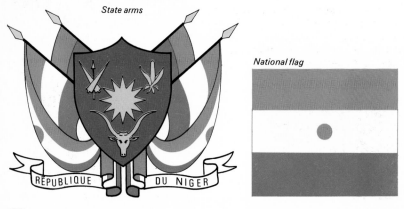

State arms

National flag

126

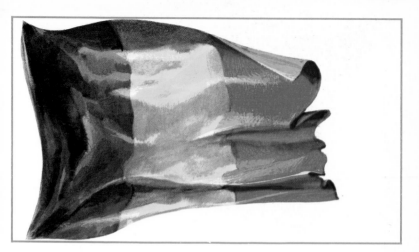

The Republic of Chad adopted its flag in 1959. Like those of several other African states that used to be administered by France, the Chad flag is inspired by the French Tricolour.

Blue stands for the sky, hope, and the southern region of the country. Yellow represents the sun and the northern region. Red stands for the national spirit and progress.

The African character of the state is intentionally stressed by the figure of the young woman shown on the state seal. The coat of arms does not make particular reference, however, to local traditions.

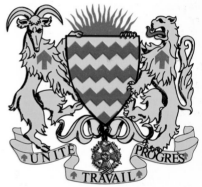

State arms

State seal

National flag

127

Sudan

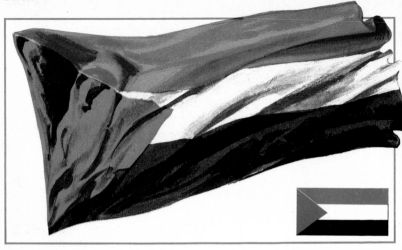

Sudan is located in northeast Africa. In 1899 it came under joint Egyptian and British control.

A horizontal tricolour—blue, yellow, and green—was adopted when the country achieved independence on January 1, 1956, but it was replaced after the 1969 revolution. The new flag was officially adopted on May 20, 1970. It was patterned after the Egyptian flag to express the new regime's pan-Arab policies. Red stands for the socialist revolution and the blood of patriots. White stands for peace and refers to the flag adopted in the 1924 revolution. Black refers to the name of the country. Sudan means "black" in Arabic, and part of Sudan is in black Africa. Green stands for prosperity and is a typical Islamic colour.

The secretary bird, indigenous to Sudan, appears in the state arms. The two inscriptions are the name of the state and the motto "Victory Is Ours."

State arms

Presidential flag

128

Ethiopia was the first independent African state. Since the late nineteenth century, the Ethiopian flag has been green, yellow, and red. These colours have come to be known as the pan-African colours, because several African countries have adopted them since the 1950s. The colours have deep roots in Ethiopia. They were originally connected with the liturgy of the Coptic Church and were considered symbols of the Trinity and the theological virtues (Faith, Hope, and Charity). Another interpretation sees the green as symbolic of the earth and its products, yellow of natural resources and peace, and red of the valour of the Ethiopian people in defending their freedom. The imperial coat of arms, with the Lion of Judah, the emperor's symbol, was abolished when the republic was proclaimed on March 21, 1975.

State arms

Djibouti

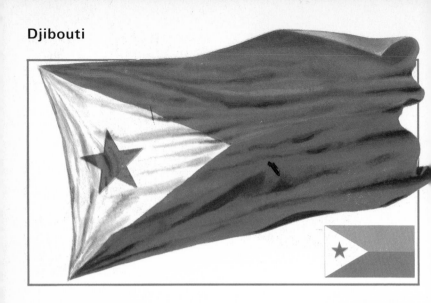

In the nineteenth century, France occupied and unified small states on the African coast at the southern end of the Red Sea. Known as the Coast of the Somalis and later as the Territory of the Afars and Issas, this country finally became independent as the Republic of Djibouti. The national flag was hoisted on Independence Day, June 27, 1977.

The basic design was originally created as a party flag by the People's African League for Independence. Similar flags were used by other political parties in the pre-independence period. The triangle is a symbol of equality, the colour white a symbol of peace. Unity is suggested by the red star. The stripes refer to the main populations of the territory. The Afars are Muslims, as indicated by the green stripe, while the Issas are a Somali people. Light blue is found in the national flag of Somalia. It is also said that the blue stands for the sea and sky, the green for earth.

The coat of arms of Djibouti features a local shield, hands holding knives, a spear, and the star of unity. The emblem is framed by a wreath and suggests the defense of the country.

State arms

Somalia

Somalia was formed by the union of British Somaliland and Italian Somalia. The new state achieved full independence, under the auspices of the United Nations, on July 1, 1960. The flag has been used since 1954. The blue field is derived from the United Nations flag. The star is a symbol of liberty, and the five points of the star stand for the five regions inhabited by Somalis: Somaliland, the former Italian Somalia, the Territory of the Afars and Issas (i.e., Djibouti), and parts of Ethiopia (Ogaden) and Kenya.

The colours of the flag reappear in the state coat of arms. The crown, which may date from Italian colonial times, is a symbol of independence.

State arms

National flag

Senegal

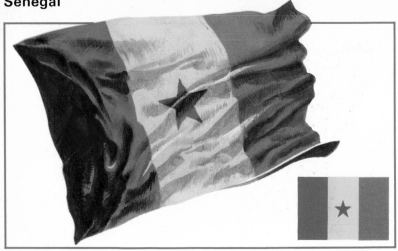

Senegal became independent in 1960. Before that it was briefly associated with Mali (then called Soudan) in the Mali Federation. When the country left the federation with Mali, the flag of the latter was adopted; however, its central emblem was replaced by a green star, the symbol of African freedom. The pan-African colours reflect the country's support of the idea of African unity. The vertical arrangement of the tricolour reflects the flag's derivation from the French Tricolour.

The shield of the coat of arms bears a lion, symbol of strength, and a baobab, Senegal's national tree. The wavy line represents the Senegal River, for which the country is named. The motto is the same as that of Mali, "One People, One Aim, One Faith." The badge is the National Order of the Republic.

State arms

Gambia is surrounded on three sides by Senegal; it fronts on the Atlantic Ocean. Gambia is one of the smallest of the African states, and its borders are the result of Anglo-French colonial disputes. Gambia became an independent state in 1965 and adopted its flag the same year. The blue band in the flag represents the Gambia River, for which the country is named. Red and green symbolize the sun and agriculture, respectively. The two white stripes stand for peace and purity.

The palm, axe, and hoe of the coat of arms also reflect the importance of agriculture in the national economy. The two lions supporting the shield are symbols of nobility and proud daring.

State arms

National flag

Guinea-Bissau

State arms

National flag

Guinea-Bissau unilaterally proclaimed independence on November 24, 1973, and Portugal recognized the new state a year later. The flag, which was adopted in 1973, is that of the African Party for the Independence of Guinea and Cape Verde. It was this party that successfully brought to an end the struggle against the Portuguese colonial regime.

The party and its role in the nation are symbolized by the black star. Following common practice in the new African countries, the colours represent the physical features (forest, savannahs, etc.) of the various geographical regions of the country.

The national coat of arms carries the colours of the flag and the motto "Unity, Struggle, Progress."

The flag of Guinea was adopted in 1958, and it is another example of the influence of the French Tricolour on African flags. Red, yellow, and green stand for the self-sacrifice of the people during the struggle for freedom, the sun and the riches of the earth, and the country's vegetation, respectively. The symbolic content of the three colours is reinforced by close association with the three words of the national motto, "Work, Justice, Solidarity."

The dove with olive branch in the state coat of arms is a traditional symbol of peace. The elephant stands for the Democratic Party of Guinea, which led the country to independence.

State arms

National flag

Sierra Leone

State arms

National flag

The Sierra Leone flag was flown for the first time on the day the country became independent, April 27, 1961. It is a horizontal tricolour, and the colours are green, white, and cobalt blue. Green is the traditional colour of agriculture, but in Sierra Leone it also stands for the hilly countryside, a typical feature of the state. White is the symbol of peace and justice. Blue stands for the Atlantic Ocean, which washes the coast.

The lion in the shield of the coat of arms is a specific reference to the name of the country and its past connection with Great Britain. The wavy blue lines and the three torches symbolize the sea and freedom achieved through knowledge. The two palm trees reflect the importance of palm oil in the national economy.

State arms

Presidential flag

Liberia was first settled in 1822 by the American Colonization Society. The country was established to provide a new home for freed slaves who wished to return to Africa. Liberia became an independent nation in 1847 and adopted a flag similar to that of the United States. The red and white stripes stand for the eleven men who signed Liberia's declaration of independence. The five-pointed star refers to the fact that, at the time of its foundation, Liberia was the only independent nation in black Africa. The blue field stands for the continent of Africa.

In the state coat of arms, the dove with the scroll is a message of peace and goodwill. The rising sun and the ship approaching the land commemorate the birth of a new nation. The plow and the hoe refer to the working of the earth, and the palm tree is a symbol of fertility. The inscription above reads: "The Love of Liberty Brought Us Here."

Counties of Liberia

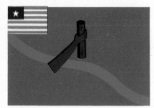

Lofa

Grand Cape Mount

Bong

Montserrado

Grand Gedeh

Grand Bassa

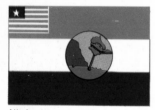

Nimba

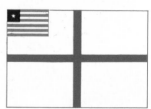

Sinoe

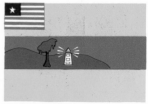

Maryland

The flag of the Ivory Coast, which is modelled after the French Tricolour, was adopted officially in 1959. Orange stands for progress and the northern part of the country. Green signifies hope and the forests of the south. White stands for the unity of the country.

The elephant in the state coat of arms is the symbol of the Democratic Party of the Ivory Coast, the party that led the country to independence. The elephant's tusk represents the origin of the country's name. The Ivory Coast flag is similar to that of Ireland. The colours are in a different order, and the proportions are different.

National flag

State arms

Ghana

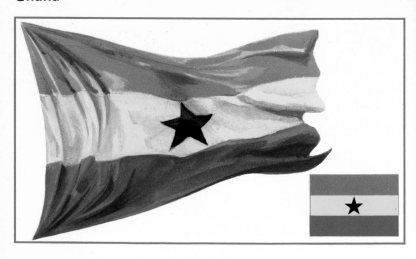

Ghana has been independent since 1957. Ghana adopted colours that have come to be known as pan-African. Red stands for the revolution and those who fought for independence. The country's natural resources are represented by the yellow stripe. (Ghana was formerly called the Gold Coast.) Green stands for the country's agricultural resources. The black star is the symbol of African freedom.

The state coat of arms has a baton, a sword, and a castle as symbols of authority. The cocoa tree and the mine stand for agriculture and natural resources. The motto is "Freedom and Justice."

The lion in the center of the shield, as well as the war ensign and civil ensign, reflect Ghana's association with Great Britain.

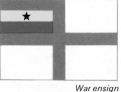

War ensign

Civil ensign

State arms

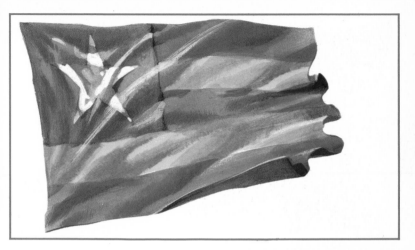

The Republic of Togo was formerly a French-administered territory. The country achieved full independence on April 27, 1960.

The flag was first hoisted on the day Togo became independent. The emerald green stripes stand for hope and the products of the earth, and the yellow stripes signify work and the country's mineral resources. The red field commemorates the martyrs for freedom and is also a symbol of love and fidelity. The white star stands for wisdom and hope.

The two lions in the coat of arms stand for the courage of the people, while the bow and arrows reflect the country's determination to defend itself from its enemies. The motto is "Work, Freedom, Fatherland."

National flag

State arms

Benin

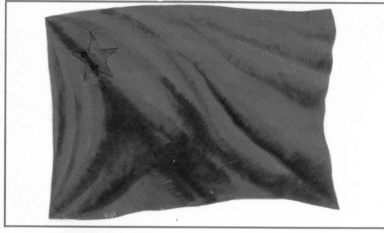

State arms

Benin is one of the smallest states in Africa. The former Dahomey, it is located between the Niger River and the Atlantic Ocean. It achieved full independence from France in 1960.

The great variety and diversity of cultural traditions of the populations that live in Benin (the successors of local kingdoms) are probably among the causes of the political instability that has marked the country's recent history.

The flag was adopted in 1975. The red star in the new flag reflects the country's adoption of Communist ideology, which was fostered by President Mathieu Kérékou. The green field stands for agriculture, the main source of national income.

National flag

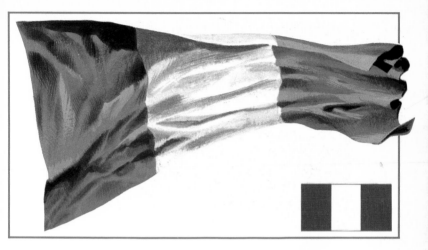

Nigeria was first a British protectorate and then a colony. Modern Nigeria was born in 1914 with the union of the southern and northern regions. It became independent in 1960 and joined the Commonwealth.

The flag was selected during a competition in which almost 3,000 designs were submitted. The simple but effective design of Michael Taiwo Akinkunmi was adopted in 1960. The green bands stand for agriculture, the country's chief source of wealth; the white stands for peace and unity.

The coat of arms was adopted in 1960. The black ground of the shield signifies the area's fertility. The Y-shaped figure represents the two rivers, Niger and Benue, which join in the middle of the country. The horses and the eagle stand for dignity and strength, respectively.

State arms

Presidential flag

143

Cameroon

National flag

State arms

The Federal Republic of Cameroon came into being in 1961, when French Cameroun (which became independent in 1960) and the former British Cameroons were united. The new nation adopted a green, red, and yellow tricolour. The federal nature of the state was referred to by two stars on the green band. The 1972 referendum reorganized the administration of Cameroon, and in 1975 the two stars were replaced by a single star on the central band.

Green stands for hope and the vegetation of the southern region. Yellow signifies the sun and the northern part of the country. Red stands for the union of the two regions.

The red section of the coat of arms, charged with a map of the country, represents Mount Cameroon. The sword and scales stand for justice and unity. The two stars commemorate the two regions that were united to form the nation.

Central African Republic

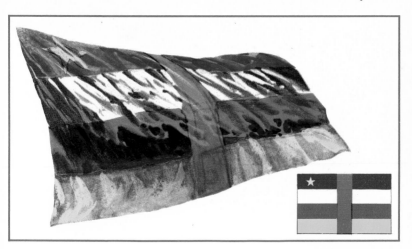

The flag of the Central African Republic was adopted in 1958. Its design is unique. The star stands for freedom. The pan-African colours—red, green, and yellow—and those of the French Tricolour express the spirit of fraternity and cooperation that should inspire relations between Africa and Europe. This hope is also reflected in the motto *Zo kwe Zo* ("A Man Is a Man") expressing the belief in the equality of all men.

A map of the country is shown beneath the star in the center of the coat of arms. The black hand in the fourth quarter commemorates MESAN, an organization that was active before independence in working for the improvement of social conditions for Africans.

State arms

Presidential flag

145

São Tomé and Príncipe

As indicated by the name of the country, São Tomé and Príncipe consists of two islands. They are located at the inner curve of the West African coast. The two black stars on the national flag stand for the islands. The colours of the flag are those of many African national flags. Specifically, in this case the red stands for the blood of those heroes who died in the struggle for national liberation. Yellow is a reminder of cacao and its importance to national income. This and the other vegetation which characterizes the islands are symbolized by the green stripes. Black symbolizes that São Tomé and Príncipe is part of black Africa.

For many years Portugal dominated the country. Independence was achieved on July 12, 1975, when the flag was first officially hoisted. The flag was created by the Movement for the Liberation of São Tomé and Príncipe, which led the independence struggle.

"Unity, Discipline, Work" is the national motto, and it appears on a ribbon at the bottom of the coat of arms. The name of the country (in Portuguese) is inscribed on the top ribbon. Native birds are supporters to the shield, which shows a tree.

State arms

A former Spanish colony, Equatorial Guinea achieved full independence on October 12, 1968. The present flag was hoisted the same day. The blue triangle by the staff represents the sea, which joins the continental regions with the islands. Green, white, and red stand for agriculture, peace, and the struggle for independence, respectively. The silk-cotton or God tree is very common in the forests of the country and was originally the emblem of Bata, the capital of the province of Rio Muni. The six stars stand for the mainland territory and the five islands that comprise the state.

State arms

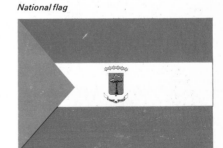

National flag

147

Gabon

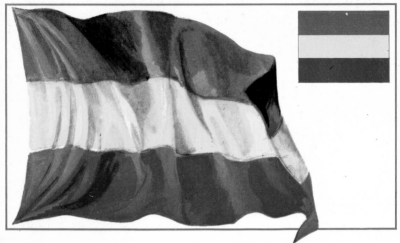

State arms

Presidential flag

The flag that Gabon adopted in 1959 had a narrower yellow stripe than the present flag, and there was a French Tricolour in the canton. Green stands for the forests, yellow for the sun, and blue for the sea.

The state coat of arms, adopted in 1963, was designed by Louis Mühlemann, a Swiss heraldic specialist. The okume tree and the three golden disks stand for the forest and mineral resources of Gabon, respectively. The ship with the national flag refers to progress and the economic importance of maritime activity. The two panthers supporting the shield are symbolic of the local population.

Two mottoes appear in the coat of arms: "United We Shall Advance" and "Unity, Labour, Justice."

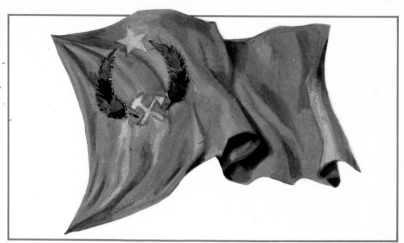

The Congo was formerly part of French Equatorial Africa and became an overseas territory in 1946. It became an independent republic within the French community in 1958 and achieved full independence in 1960.

In 1958 Congo adopted a flag in which the pan-African colours— green, yellow, and red—were arranged in diagonal stripes. The socialist revolution began in 1963, and in 1969 Congo became a people's republic. The new flag has been in use since 1970. The star stands for hope, the palm branches for peace, and the hammer and hoe (instead of the usual sickle) stand for the unity of workers and peasants. Red, the universal colour of Communism, also refers to the people's resistance to the French during the years of colonialism.

National flag

Zaire

The former Belgian Congo has been an independent republic since 1960. Zaire adopted its new name and a new flag in 1971. The pan-African colours reflect the country's support of African collaboration.

The figure in the yellow disk, an arm with a torch, is derived from the emblem of the People's Revolutionary Movement.

The coat of arms contains a leopard head, a crossed spear and arrow, a palm branch, and an elephant tusk. The motto below reads: "Justice, Peace, Labour."

The president of Zaire is also the commander of the armed forces. Hence the standard shows both modern instruments of war together with traditional local weapons.

State arms

Presidential flag

The Republic of Uganda has been independent since October 9, 1962. The new flag was hoisted the same day. The crested crane was originally part of the colonial emblem. The colours of the flag—black, yellow, and red—stand for the people of Africa, the sun, and brotherhood, respectively.

The coat of arms was adopted in 1962. The heraldic symbols of water stand for Lake Victoria and the source of the Nile. The sun, symbolic of the Equator, refers to Uganda's geographical position. Former kingdoms in the territory are symbolized by the drum, a traditional symbol of royal authority. Coffee and cotton are shown below and reflect the importance of these products in the national economy.

State arms

Presidential flag

Rwanda

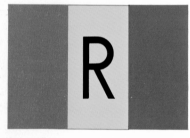

National flag

State arms

Rwanda has been independent since 1962. Before then it was part of the Belgian trust territory of Ruanda-Urundi.

The red, yellow, and green of the flag are pan-African colours. Red stands for the struggle for independence, yellow for peace, and green for hope. This flag was adopted the year before Rwanda won independence. The letter R stands for the name of the state and is the only element that distinguishes the flag of Rwanda from that of Guinea. The R also refers to the 1961 referendum that resulted in the establishment of a republican government.

The dove with the olive branch in the coat of arms is a symbol of peace. The hoe and sickle stand for the working of the earth. The bow and arrow symbolize the country's defense of its freedom.

Burundi

Burundi became independent in 1962 and adopted a flag with a drum in the center as a symbol of royal authority. The flag that was adopted in 1967, after the *coup d'état* which made the state a republic, is charged with three stars, which refer to the words of the national motto, "Unity, Work, Progress," inscribed on the coat of arms. Red stands for those who fell in the cause of independence, green for hope, and white for peace.

The three spears in the coat of arms, like the stars on the flag, refer to the state's motto. The lion dates to the colonial period and has been maintained by the republic.

National flag

State arms

153

Tanzania

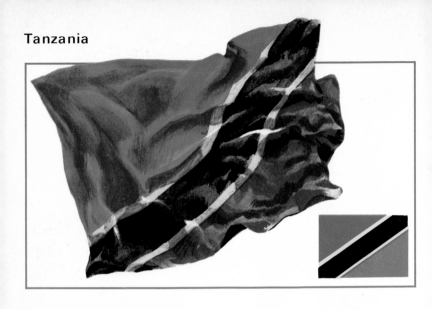

State arms

The United Republic of Tanzania was born in 1964 with the union of Tanganyika and Zanzibar. This union is reflected in the flag adopted on June 30, 1964. The flag of Tanganyika consisted of two green bands with a black one in between, symbolizing the fertility of the earth and the largest ethnic component of the country. When Tanganyika became independent in 1961, two thin yellow stripes were added to symbolize the mineral resources of the country. Zanzibar, which became independent in 1963, had a blue, black, and green tricolour. When the two countries joined to form Tanzania, a blue band was added to the flag of Tanganyika, and the colours were arranged diagonally.

The main elements of the state coat of arms are the torch of freedom and Mount Kilimanjaro with coffee and cotton plants. The motto in Swahili can be translated "Freedom and Unity."

Presidential flag

Kenya

A British protectorate in 1890 and a colony in 1920, Kenya won full independence in 1963.

The flag adopted in 1963 is derived from that of the Kenya African National Union, the political movement that led the country to independence. Black and red stand for the African population and its blood, which is like that of all other humans. The earth and its resources are symbolized by green. The two white stripes, which were added when the country became independent, stand for peace. The Masai shield and the two spears symbolize the defense of freedom, which cost so many years of struggle.

The shield of the coat of arms is supported by two lions and shows a cock with an axe, the emblem of the Kenya African National Union (KANU). Mount Kenya is depicted covered with agricultural products, including coffee, tea, chamomile, and sisal. The Swahili inscription reads: "Let Us Work Together."

State arms

155

Seychelles

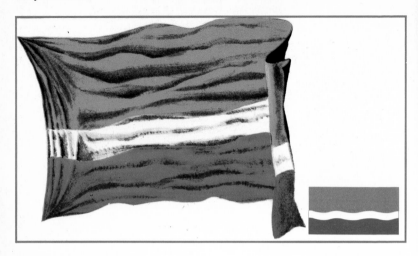

The nineteenth-century British imperialist General Charles Gordon chose the symbols shown in the coat of arms of the Seychelles. The palm tree is a species found only on those islands, known as the *coco-de-mer*. The giant tortoise, white-tailed trop-

State arms

ical bird, and sailfish are also characteristic of the wildlife found in the Seychelles. The Latin motto translates "The End Crowns the Work."

Independence was achieved by the Seychelles in 1976 following decades of British colonial domination. A revolution the following year introduced a new national flag, which is still in use. The basic design is similar to the party flag of the Seychelles People's United Party which organized the revolution.

The broad red stripe at the top is a symbol of revolution and progress, while the green at the bottom indicates the Seychellois people rely on agriculture for their livelihood. The white wavy stripe symbolizes the resources of the Indian Ocean, where the Seychelles Islands are located, and the beautiful beaches of the islands. Seychelles is one of the two countries in the world (Kiribati being the other) with a national flag in which the stripes are wavy rather than straight.

The British Crown Colony of St. Helena, which comprises the islands of St. Helena, Ascension, and Tristan da Cunha and other smaller islands, is located in the south central Atlantic.

St. Helena was discovered by the Portuguese navigator João da Nova Castell in 1502. This uninhabited island was visited by Thomas Cavendish during his round-the-world voyage in the *Desire*. It became a staging port on the sea routes between Europe and India and was annexed to Holland in 1633. The island was occupied by John Dutton on behalf of the British East India Company. It belonged to the Company (except from 1815 to 1821, when Napoleon was exiled there) until 1834, when it became a crown colony.

The flag is the British Blue Ensign charged with the colonial badge. The badge shows a sailing ship flying the cross of St. George approaching two promontories.

Badge

State and war ensign

157

Angola

After centuries of Portuguese colonial domination, Angola became an independent nation on November 11, 1975. The national flag was hoisted at that time. It contains symbols of the revolutionary Popular Movement for the Liberation of Angola, which was in the forefront of the struggle to end colonial rule.

State arms

The red stripe is for the liberation struggle; the black stands for an independent black African nation. The machete and cogwheel represent the agricultural and industrial workers of the country, united to help Angola progress. The star stands for internationalism and advancement, its five points suggesting unity, liberty, justice, democracy, and progress. The flag of the Popular Movement for the Liberation of Angola was similar except that the star was larger and the machete and cogwheel were omitted.

The three symbols of the flag also appear in the national coat of arms. In addition, there is a traditional African hoe and typical Angolan products—corn, cotton, and coffee. The open book is a symbol of education and culture, important for the development of the nation, which is symbolized by the rising sun. The name of the country appears in Portuguese on the ribbon at the bottom of the coat of arms.

Zambia

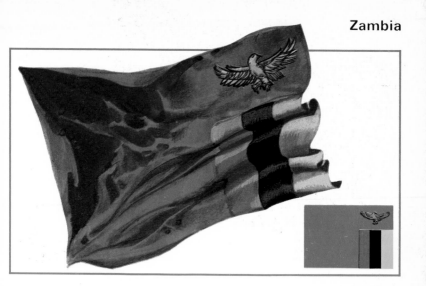

The Zambian flag was adopted in 1964, at the time the country became independent. Its colours are derived from the flag of the UNIP, the United Party of National Independence. The green field stands for agriculture. Red stands for the struggle for freedom, black for the population of Zambia, and orange for the country's mineral resources. The eagle stands for the conquest of freedom and the nation's hopes for the future.

The state coat of arms is modelled after the emblem that was granted when Zambia was still the colony of Northern Rhodesia. Victoria Falls are represented in the shield. The country's natural resources are referred to by the mining installation, the corn cob, and the zebra. The country's motto is "One Zambia, One Nation."

Presidential flag

State arms

Malawi

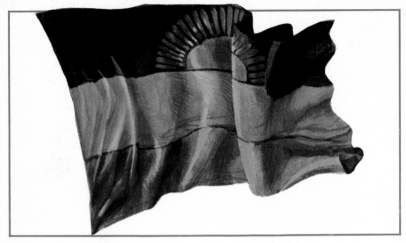

State arms

National flag

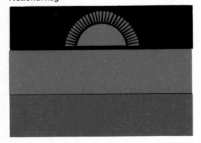

Malawi's flag was adopted in 1964, the year the country achieved independence. It is a horizontal tricolour. The colours are black, red, and green; there is a rising sun in the center of the black band. A flag like this one, but without the rising sun, was used by the Malawi Congress Party from 1953 on. The Congress Party led the country to independence.

Black stands for the African people, red for the blood of those who fought for freedom, and green for the country's fertility. The rising sun was added in 1964 as a symbol of a new era for the whole African continent.

The lion in the center of the shield reflects the fact that Malawi is a member of the Commonwealth. The heraldic symbol for water refers to Lake Nyasa. The sun is shown as it was on the coat of arms when the country was the colony of Nyasaland. The lion, leopard, and eagle are typical local fauna. Mount Mlanje is in the compartment at the base of the coat of arms.

Mozambique

Vasco da Gama reached the coast of what is now Mozambique in 1498. Mozambique was gradually colonized by the Portuguese, who were interested in the rich interior regions of the country. Although Portuguese interest declined in the eighteenth century, it revived in the nineteenth. Mozambique achieved independence on June 25, 1975, under the leadership of the FRELIMO, the Mozambique Liberation Front.

The first flag, adopted in 1974, was that of the FRELIMO. A new flag was introduced later. It had the same colours, but they were arranged differently. The colours stand for the blood shed in the struggle for independence, the products of agriculture, and the country's mineral resources. The cogwheel, the hoe, and the book symbolize workers, farmers, and intellectuals. The red star stands for independence and the state's political creed. The rifle stands for the country's defense of its freedom.

National flag

State arms

161

Comoros

State arms

National flag

This archipelago in the Indian Ocean, northwest of Madagascar, became the Republic of the Comoros on July 6, 1975, having been a French overseas territory. The islands first appeared on a map in the early sixteenth century, and the Englishman James Lancaster reached the Comoros about 1590. The islands were long dominated by the Arabs. In the nineteenth century they became a French protectorate, at first together with Madagascar (1914). In 1947 the Comoros became an overseas territory. A large degree of autonomy was granted in 1960.

While other French overseas territories used the Tricolour, the Comoros adopted its own flag in 1963, of which the present flag is an adaptation. The crescent and the colour green are symbolic of Islam, and most of the inhabitants of the Comoros are Muslim. The four stars stand for the larger islands of the archipelago: Grande Comore, Mayotte (which the French still occupy), Anjouan, and Mohéli.

Malagasy Republic (Madagascar)

The first Europeans reached Madagascar in the sixteenth century. From the sixteenth century until the nineteenth century, Madagascar was one of the centers of the African slave trade. It became a French colony in 1896 and achieved independence in 1960.

The flag, which was adopted in 1959, is derived in part from the white and red flags used by the Hovas, who used to play a dominant role on the island. It should also be noted that during past centuries Madagascar received many immigrants from Southeast Asia, and red and white are common colours in that area. The green band stands for the inhabitants of the areas washed by the Indian Ocean.

The state coat of arms carries the name of the country and the motto "Fatherland, Revolution, Liberty." A rising sun, weapons, and agricultural produce complete the design.

State arms

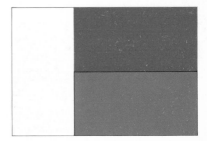

National flag

Mauritius

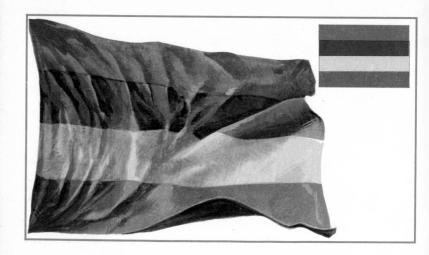

The flag was adopted in 1968, the year the country achieved independence. Red stands for the martyrs of independence, blue for the sea, yellow for freedom, and green for the fertility of the earth.

The coat of arms dates from 1906 and was confirmed after independence. The ship in the quartered shield refers to the first colonizers; the three palm trees stand for the local vegetation; while the key and star illustrate the Latin motto "The Star and the Key of the Indian Ocean," referring to the island's strategic positions. A sambar and dodo bird support the shield; they hold sugar canes.

State ensign

Civil ensign

State arms

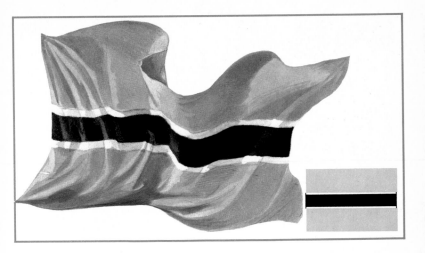

The former British protectorate of Bechuanaland became independent Botswana in 1966. Botswana is a member of the Commonwealth. The flag, adopted in 1966, symbolizes the equality and unity of the black and white populations under the country's blue sky.

The three cogwheels and the bull's head in the coat of arms stand for industry and animal husbandry. The sorghum refers to agriculture, and the two zebras and the elephant tusk stand for the local fauna. The zebra is an important symbol, for its black and white stripes stand for the same racial cooperation that is symbolized in the national flag.

The vital importance of rain is symbolized by the water sign and the word *pula* (meaning "rain"), which is also used as a greeting.

State arms

Presidential flag

Zimbabwe

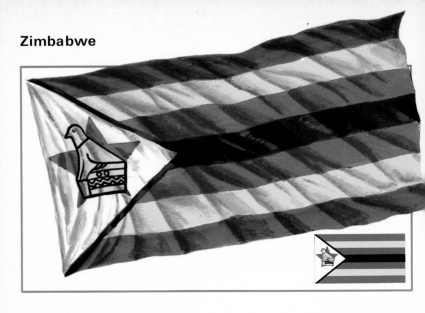

Zimbabwe, previously Rhodesia, heralded its independence on April 18, 1980 by hoisting a new national flag. The seven stripes are taken from the flag of concentric rectangles of black, red, yellow, and green that had been used by the Zimbabwe African National Union. This political party, part

State arms

of the Patriotic Front, was under the leadership of Robert Mugabe, who became the first prime minister of Zimbabwe. Black stands for the African majority of the population, red for the blood shed in the liberation struggle, yellow for mineral wealth, green for vegetation and agriculture, and white for peace. The red star is a symbol of socialism and national aspiration.

The Zimbabwe bird is a soapstone carving from an ancient African culture and thus represents the heritage of the past. It also appears in the crest of the Rhodesian coat of arms, which has not yet been replaced by a new design. Created in 1924, the arms show a lion and two thistles taken from the personal arms of nineteenth-century British imperialist Cecil Rhodes for whom the country was then named. A pick representing mining activities and sable antelopes complete the design. The motto translates from the Latin as "May I Be Worthy of the Name."

The flag was adopted in 1927. It is an orange, white, and blue tricolour. The colours are those of the House of Orange and were introduced in South Africa by Dutch colonists in the seventeenth century. The emblem in the center of the white band

National flag

consists of three flags. The Union Jack stands for the British Cape Colony and Natal. The flag in the center (white and orange stripes with the Dutch tricolour in the canton) represents the Orange Free State. The four-coloured flag (*Vierkleur*) on the right represents the Transvaal.

In the quarters of the shield, the Cape of Good Hope is symbolized by the woman with the anchor; Natal by wild animals; the Orange Free State by the orange tree; and the Transvaal by the wagon. The crest is a lion with a bundle of rods, which refers to the country's motto "Strength in Unity."

State arms

167

South Africa

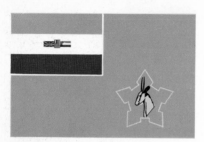

War flag

War ensign

South West Africa is controlled by South Africa, but its independence under the name Namibia is being promoted by the United Nations. It has no national flag.

KwaZulu

Provinces and Bantustans

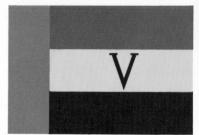

Venda

Gazan Kulu

Bophuthatswana

168

South Africa

Lebowa

Orange Free State

Transkei

Provinces and Bantustans

Transvaal

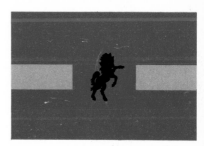

Qwaqwa

Ciskei

Swaziland

Swaziland became an autonomous state in 1967 and achieved independence within the Commonwealth in 1968. Swaziland adopted a flag in October 1967 that is derived from the standard used by the Swazis during the World War II. Blue stands for peace, yellow for mineral resources, and crimson for the battles of the past. In the center is the shield of the Emasotsha warriors, two Zulu spears, and a rod with blue widowbird plumes, which are royal ornaments.

The lion, which appears on the coat of arms and on the royal standard, and the elephant are attributes of the royal family. Their meaning is stressed by the motto "We Are the Fortress."

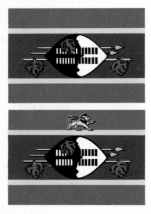

Royal flag

State and war flag

State arms

Lesotho

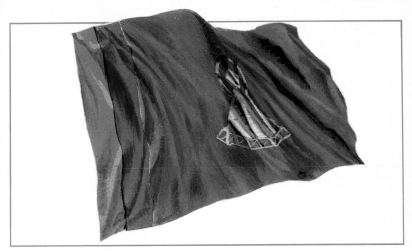

Lesotho has been independent since 1966. The colours of the national flag are derived from those used by the Lesotho National Party, the most important political movement in the country. Red stands for faith, and green for the earth. Blue represents the sky, and white symbolizes peace. The stylized hat is a traditional symbol of the Basotho people. The crocodile on the coat of arms is the emblem of the ruling dynasty. Behind the shield are typical weapons of the region. The compartment is Mount Thaba Bosiu, where King Moshoeshoe I was buried in the nineteenth century. The scroll bears the motto "Peace, Rain, Abundance."

State and war flag

State arms

North and Central America

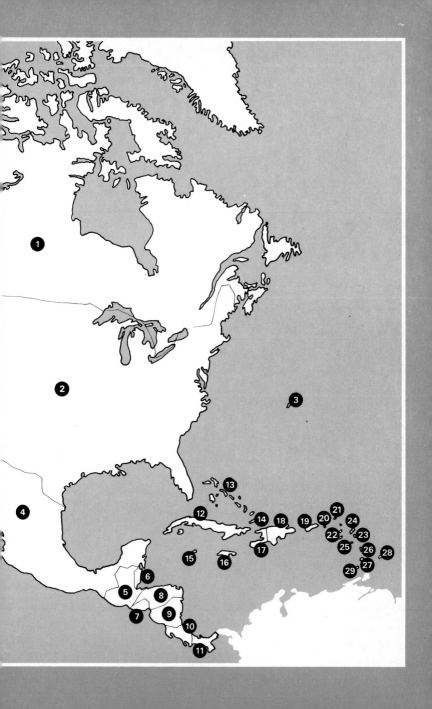

Canada

Canada did not have a distinctive national flag of its own until February 15, 1965. Before then it had flown the British Red Ensign with the Canadian coat of arms in the fly. In 1964 the then-Prime Minister, Lester Pearson, suggested that Canada have its own flag. More than four thousand suggestions were submitted. Since 1921 red and white have been Canada's national colours, and they also appear in the dominion's coat of arms. The maple leaf has been the emblem of Canada for more than a century.

The composite nature of the dominion is reflected in the coat of arms. The shield shows the arms of four countries that colonized Canada: England, Scotland, Ireland, and France. The supporters are the British lion and the Scottish unicorn. The French banner also appears. The lion on the helm has a maple leaf and commemorates those who fell in World War I. The Latin motto can be translated "From Sea to Sea."

State arms

Canada

National flag

*Queen Elizabeth's
personal flag for Canada*

Provinces and territories

Northwest Territories

Yukon

British Columbia

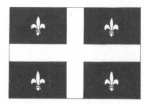

Quebec

Newfoundland

Manitoba

Provinces and territories

Alberta

Saskatchewan

Ontario

Prince Edward Island

New Brunswick

Nova Scotia

The present version of the American flag, the twenty-eighth, was first hoisted on July 4, 1960. A resolution that Congress passed in 1818 provides that the number of stars in the blue canton correspond to the number of states in the union. The fiftieth state (Hawaii) became a part of the union in 1959. The thirteen stripes stand for the thirteen original states. It is still not certain how the stars and stripes were originally created. It is clear, however, that British flags, which were common in the colonies, provided the starting point for the basic design (with the canton at the upper left) and for the colours. The first flag (1776) was the British Red Ensign with red and white stripes instead of the solid red field. In 1777 the Union Jack in the canton was replaced by thirteen stars. The number of stars in the canton has been changed as new states joined the union.

The coat of arms dates from 1782. The pattern on the shield is a variation

National flag

State arms

177

United States of America

Presidential flag

of the design of the national flag. The American eagle holds an olive branch in one talon and thirteen arrows in the other. These are symbols of peace and war, but the number thirteen also refers to the original colonies.

State flags of the United States

Alaska

Washington

Montana

North Dakota

State flags of the United States

Minnesota

Wisconsin

Michigan

New York

Vermont

Maine

New Hampshire

Massachusetts

179

State flags of the United States

Rhode Island

Connecticut

Oregon (obverse)

Idaho

Wyoming

South Dakota

Nebraska

Iowa

State flags of the United States

Illinois

Indiana

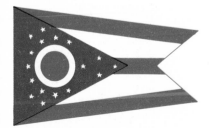

Ohio

Pennsylvania

New Jersey

Delaware

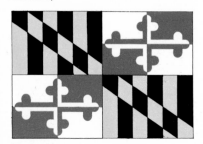

Maryland

California

State flags of the United States

Nevada

Utah

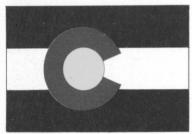

Colorado

Kansas

Missouri

Kentucky

District of Columbia

Virginia

State flags of the United States

West Virginia

Arizona

New Mexico

Oklahoma

Arkansas

Mississippi

Alabama

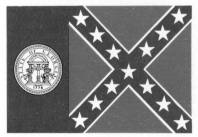

Georgia

State flags of the United States

South Carolina

Tennessee

North Carolina

Texas

Louisiana

Florida

Hawaii

Bermuda

The British Crown Colony of
Bermuda consists of about three
hundred islands in the Atlantic Ocean
to the east of the United States. The
islands were probably discovered by
the Spanish explorer Juan de
Bermúdez, for whom Bermuda is
named, in the early sixteenth century.
These uninhabited islands were
colonized by the survivors of the
shipwreck of the *Sea Venture*, who
called them the Somers Islands in
honour of Admiral George Somers.

The lion in the coat of arms holds a
shield depicting the shipwreck of the
Sea Venture in 1609. The ship
foundered on an underwater reef.

Bermuda is the only British colony
that adopted the Red Ensign instead
of the Blue as its local flag on land.
This may have been because the first
settlers arrived on board merchant
ships flying the Red Ensign.

State arms

Civil flag and ensign

185

Mexico

Mexico has been independent since 1821 and adopted a green, white, and red tricolour. This flag derives from the flag of the "Three Guarantees," flown during the war of independence from Spain.

White, green, and red stand for religion, independence, and the unity of the Mexican states (the three guarantees).

The order of the colours was established in 1823. The size of the flag and the details of the state coat of arms were established in 1968, on the occasion of the Olympic Games in Mexico City. The state coat of arms refers to the legendary foundation of Tenochtitlán (modern Mexico City). According to this tradition, the Aztecs were to build a city when they found a lake with an island in the middle and a cactus plant growing on it. An eagle with a serpent in its beak perched on the cactus plant as a sign to the Aztecs.

National flag

State arms

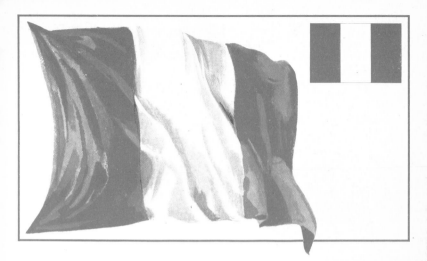

The current flag of Guatemala was officially adopted in 1968. Like those of El Salvador, Honduras, Nicaragua, and Costa Rica, the flag of Guatemala is derived from the former United Provinces of the Center of America (Central American federation), which was established in 1821 when Spanish colonial dominion ended.

The colours and their arrangement reflect the geographical situation of Guatemala, washed by the waters of the Pacific Ocean on the west and by the Caribbean Sea on the east. The choice of the flag also reflects the hope that the association of states that formed the federation can one day be revived.

The bird in the state emblem is the *quetzal* (*Paramocrus mocinno*), the traditional bird of freedom. The date on the scroll, September 15, 1821, is the day Guatemala became independent. The rifles and swords symbolize the defense of the country's freedom.

State arms

State and war flag and ensign

187

Belize

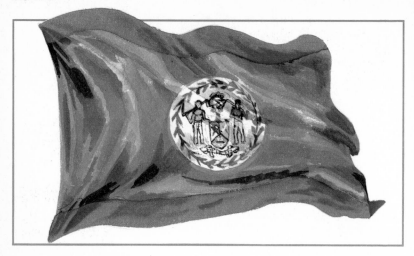

State arms

National flag

Belize was formerly known as British Honduras and flew the usual colonial flags until independence on September 21, 1981. In addition, however, Belize used an unofficial national flag following the attainment of self-government in 1964. It was blue with the traditional coat of arms on a central white disk.

The coat of arms, officially recognized in 1907, dates to 1819. The shield shows the tools used in the logging industry which provided most of the income of Belize until recently. The supporters of the shield (a Mestizo and a Creole) also hold an axe and a paddle. The crest is a mahogany tree, as referred to in the motto "I Flourish in the Shade." The shield also shows a representation of a ship, such as was used by the buccaneers of the early seventeenth century. Since independence the national flag of Belize has been modified. Red, the colour of the United Democratic Party, was added in 1981 at the top and bottom.

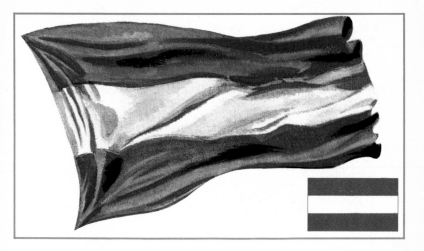

The flag of El Salvador was originally adopted in 1821 by the Central American federation, of which El Salvador was a state. El Salvador used this blue-white-blue tricolour until 1865, when it adopted a flag with stars and stripes similar to that of the United States. The older flag was revived in 1912 to honour the old federation. The two blue bands stand for the Caribbean Sea and the Pacific Ocean.

Within the triangle of the state emblem, a symbol of equality and freedom, are a rainbow, a Phrygian cap referring to liberty, and five volcanoes rising between two bodies

State arms

of water, the Atlantic and Pacific oceans. The date, September 15, 1821, is that of El Salvador's independence from Spain.

State flag; war flag and ensign

Civil ensign; war flag; state flag and ensign

Honduras

Honduras achieved independence in 1821 as part of the Central American federation along with El Salvador, Costa Rica, Nicaragua, and Guatemala. The present flag, which was officially adopted in 1949, is similar to that of the federation, which came to an end in the years 1838 to 1839.

The blue bands stand for the Caribbean Sea and the Pacific Ocean. The five stars, introduced in 1866, reflect the hope that the five states may once again form an association.

The Masonic triangle in the state emblem stands for equality and justice. The two towers represent independence and sovereignty. The arrows at the top commemorate the indigenous population. The two cornucopias at the sides stand for the country's natural resources. The trees, mines, and equipment below symbolize the forest and the mineral resources of the country.

War ensign

State arms

Nicaragua

When Nicaragua became independent of Spain in 1821, it was united with four other countries (El Salvador, Costa Rica, Guatemala, and Honduras) in the Central American federation.

The present version of its flag dates from 1971 and is almost identical with the one the federation used from 1823 to 1839, the year it came to an end.

The blue bands round a white one stand for the geographical position of Nicaragua between the Pacific Ocean and the Caribbean Sea. The state emblem dates from 1908 and resembles that of the original federation. The triangle is a symbol of equality and justice. The rainbow stands for hope, and the Phrygian cap for liberty. The five volcanoes rising between two bodies of water commemorate the five countries that formed the United Provinces of the Center of America.

State arms

National flag

Costa Rica

When Costa Rica achieved independence from Spain in 1821, it joined the United Provinces of the Center of America. Costa Rica withdrew from the federation in 1838. The flag that was most recently modified on October 21, 1964, is essentially that of the old federation, from which the blue and the white are derived. The colour red dates from 1848, to commemorate the revolutionary activity in France of that year.

The inscription *America Central* on the state coat of arms refers to the old federation and the hope of one day reconstituting a supranational community. There used to be five stars, representing the member states of the federation. There are now seven, indicating the provinces of Costa Rica. The three mountains stand for the volcanoes Barba, Irazun, and Poás. The two bodies of water are the Atlantic and Pacific oceans. The rising sun stands for the dawn of a new era.

Civil ensign

State arms

Panama

Panama broke away from Colombia in 1903 and declared independence. The flag, designed by the son of the first president of the republic, Manuel Amador Guerrero, was hoisted on November 3, 1903.

The country's two historical political parties, the Liberals and the Conservatives, are represented by red and blue, respectively. White stands for the concord between the two parties. The blue star is for loyalty. The red star symbolizes the authority of the law.

In the shield's quarters, the rifle and sword stand for the civil wars in which the country's blood was shed; the tools stand for work; the cornucopia represents abundance and prosperity; and the winged wheel stands for progress. The country's geographical position, between the Pacific Ocean and the Caribbean Sea, is illustrated in the center of the shield. The nine stars symbolize the nine provinces of Panama.

State arms

National flag

Cuba

Cuba's flag was officially adopted in 1902. It was designed by Miguel Teurbe Tolón at the request of General Narcisio López, instigator of one of the first attempts to free the island from Spanish colonial rule. The blue and white stripes stand for the original provinces of Cuba and for the purity of the revolution. The red triangle symbolizes liberty, equality, and fraternity, and the blood shed in the conquest and defense of freedom. The five-pointed star, the "lone star," represents the country's independence.

The island's geographical position is illustrated in the state coat of arms. The key to the Gulf of Mexico, Cuba

State arms

Presidential flag

is in the Tropic of Cancer (the sun), between Florida and the Yucatán peninsula. The bundle of rods and the Phrygian cap above the shield are symbols of authority and liberty. The palm tree stands for the fertility of the earth. The national colours, a branch of oak, and a branch of laurel also appear in the coat of arms.

The natural features of the West Indies are the main motif in the flag that the Bahamas adopted in 1973, the year the islands became independent. The aquamarine stripes and the yellow stripe stand for the sea and the archipelago's shores. The black triangle is considered a symbol of unity. The three ensigns reflect the British past and the Bahamas' membership of the Commonwealth.

State arms

War ensign and flag

Civil ensign

State ensign

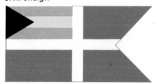

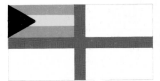

Turks and Caicos Islands

State arms

The Turks Islands were discovered about 1512, and in the second half of the seventeenth century they were colonized by settlers from Bermuda. Late in the eighteenth century, Jamaica claimed sovereignty of the islands, which, despite the opposition of the inhabitants, were annexed in 1804. After years of struggle the Turks were granted a separate administration. The Caicos, settled and then abandoned by Americans who remained loyal to Great Britain during the American Revolution, were joined to the Turks in 1848.

The crest of the coat of arms is a pelican between two sisal plants. The supporters are flamingos. The shield shows typical examples of the local flora and fauna, including a conch shell, a lobster, and a cactus.

The flag is the British Blue Ensign charged with the colony's shield.

State ensign

The Cayman Islands were discovered in 1503 by Christopher Columbus. He called them the Tortugas for the many turtles he saw. The Caymans were colonized by the British in the second half of the seventeenth century. Until 1962 the islands were a dependency of Jamaica, and then they became a separate colony with a large degree of self-government.

The crest of the coat of arms has a pineapple plant and a turtle. The shield shows the British lion and three stars over the heraldic symbol for water. The three stars stand for the islands of the archipelago: Grand Cayman, Cayman Brac, and Little

State arms

State ensign

Cayman. The flag, like those of other British colonies, consists of the British Blue Ensign charged with the colony's coat of arms.

197

Jamaica

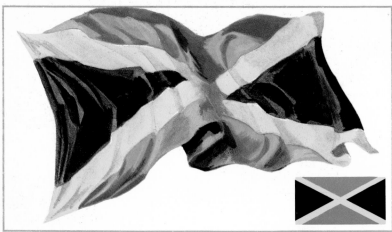

Jamaica was a British colony until 1962, when it achieved full independence. It is a member of the Commonwealth. The flag that was adopted at independence bears a yellow St. Andrew's cross that forms two green triangles and two black ones. Green stands for agriculture and the hope for the future. Black stands for the past and the obstacles the country must still overcome.

The state coat of arms is a modification of the one created in 1661. The shield is supported by two Arawak

State arms

Indians. Pineapples are depicted in the shield; they are one of the country's major agricultural resources.

Queen Elizabeth's personal flag for Jamaica

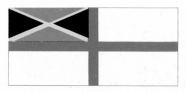

War ensign

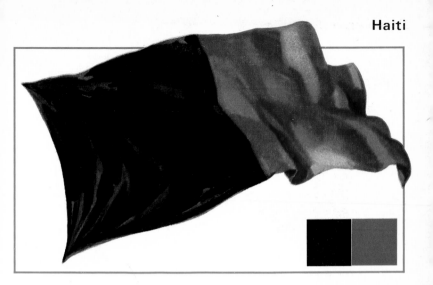

Haiti is located in the western part of the island of Hispaniola. It has been an independent republic since 1804. The first flag, derived from the French Tricolour, consisted of vertical blue and red bands. The colours stood for the black and mulatto elements of the population. Subsequently black replaced blue. In 1806 a new flag was introduced, this time with blue-and-red bands set horizontally. This version was in use until 1964. On June 21, 1964, the vertical black and red were revived.

The coat of arms was designed in 1807 by President Alexander Sabés Petion and was slightly modified in 1964. The palm tree stands for liberty. The spirit of cooperation between blacks and mulattoes in the struggle for independence is referred to in the motto "Unity Gives Strength."

State arms

State and war flag and ensign

L'UNION FAIT LA FORCE

Dominican Republic

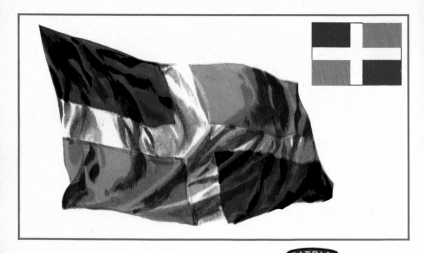

The Dominican Republic, which occupies the eastern part of the island of Hispaniola, became independent of Spain in 1821 but remained associated with Haiti until 1844. The flag that was adopted in 1844 was designed by Juan Pablo Duarte, who founded a secret society, the *Trinitaria*. It was under the lead of the *Trinitaria* that the Dominican Republic separated from Haiti and established independence. Blue and red, which already appeared in the Haitian flag, stand for freedom and the people's sacrifices in the cause of independence. The white cross

State arms

stands for the religion of the republic. Surrounded by laurel and palm branches, the shield of the state coat of arms carries the national colours as well as a cross and an open Bible, representing the Christian religion. The motto is "God, Fatherland, Freedom."

State and war flag and ensign

Puerto Rico

National flag

State arms

When Columbus landed in Puerto Rico (November 19, 1493), the island was inhabited by Indians from Florida and South America. Juan Ponce de León reached Puerto Rico in 1508 and founded the city of Caparra. Puerto Rico was one of the first sites of Spanish settlement in the Western Hemisphere. Because of its strategic position, the island was often attacked by the French, the British (1595 and 1598), and the Dutch (1625).

During the nineteenth century, Puerto Rico received a host of settlers from former Spanish colonies in South America. After the Spanish-American War of 1898, Puerto Rico was ceded to the United States. It now has internal self-government. The flag, which resembles that of Cuba, was adopted in 1895 during the revolutionary struggles against Spanish colonial domination.

It was officially recognized as the national flag in 1952 and is flown alongside the United States flag.

United States Virgin Islands

Territorial flag

State seal

These islands were discovered by Columbus in 1493, and Danish settlers arrived in the second half of the seventeenth century. They settled chiefly in St. Thomas, St. John, and St. Croix (which was acquired by France). These islands were known as the Danish West Indian Islands until 1917 when they became an American dependency. (They were twice occupied by the British, 1801–1802 and 1807–1815.)

America had tried to acquire the islands during the Civil War. The purchase was effected in 1917 for twenty-five million dollars. The islands were considered strategically important for access to the Panama Canal.

The islands have their own fifteen-person senate. Since 1932 the inhabitants have been American citizens. The flag has a white field charged with the American eagle. The letters V and I stand for Virgin Islands.

The British colony of the Virgin Islands consists of thirty-six islands in the Caribbean northeast of Puerto Rico.

The islands were discovered by Columbus in 1493 and conquered by the Spaniards in the second half of the sixteenth century. Dutch settlers arrived about the middle of the seventeenth century, and British settlement began in 1666. They were annexed to the British Leeward Islands in 1672, and in 1773 they were granted their own administration. When the colony of the Leeward Islands was dissolved in 1956, the Virgin Islands declined the invitation to join the West Indian Federation and became a crown colony.

The coat of arms shows twelve oil lamps and a virgin dressed in white. The flag is the British Blue Ensign charged with the colony's coat of arms.

State arms

State ensign

203

St. Christopher – Nevis – Anguilla

The three islands of St. Christopher (St. Kitts), Nevis, and Anguilla formed an associated state of the United Kingdom in 1967. The state is completely independent as far as internal affairs are concerned, but defense and foreign affairs are entrusted to Great Britain. A few months after the association was founded, Anguilla seceded from the association. Attempts to mediate failed, and in March 1969, Great Britain sent a military contingent to Anguilla to set up a British commission for administration. A law was proposed in 1971 that would provide a separate government for Anguilla. A new constitution was drawn up in 1976 that would make Anguilla a British dependency separate from St. Kitts and Nevis.

The present flag of the associated state is a tricolour, and the three palm branches stand for the three islands. Since 1967 Anguilla has used its own flag, which has not been recognized officially.

State arms

State and civil flag

One of the Leeward Islands in the Caribbean, Montserrat is a British colony. It declined the invitation to join the ranks of the associated states of the United Kingdom.

The island was discovered in 1493 by Christopher Columbus. Irish settlers began to arrive in the early seventeenth century.

On the coat of arms a woman with a harp is shown embracing a Latin cross.

The colony flag is the British Blue Ensign charged with the coat of arms.

State arms

State ensign

205

Antigua and Barbuda

State arms

Antigua was discovered in 1493 by Christopher Columbus, and English settlers began to arrive in the early seventeenth century. They raised tobacco and sugar cane.

Antigua was an associated state of the United Kingdom from 1967 until independence, November 1, 1981. The state includes the islands of Antigua, Barbuda, and Redonda, all part of the Leeward Islands.

The flag dates from 1967. Red and blue stand for strength and hope. Black refers to the African origin of the population. Yellow, blue, and white together stand for the islands' natural attractions. The sun symbolizes the dawn of a new era of freedom.

The crest of the coat of arms shows a pineapple plant and hibiscus flowers. The supporters are two stags with a sugar cane and an agave. The importance of sugar in the state's economy is reflected in the tower of the old sugar mill on the shield.

National flag

The flag of Dominica was hoisted on November 3, 1978—Independence Day. Dark green suggests the vegetation which covers the island. The cross is for Christianity, its three colours represent the Trinity. Yellow also stands for the Carib Indians, white for the rivers and waterfalls of Dominica, and black for the majority of the population, which is of African background. In the center is a disk of red (for socialism) with ten stars for the ten parishes of the island. The stars surround a representation of the national bird, the *sisserou* parrot. The coat of arms shows a coconut tree and a banana tree, a Dominican

National flag

toad, and a local canoe. The supporters are parrots. The inscription bears the motto "After the Good Lord, We Love the Earth."

State arms

207

St. Lucia

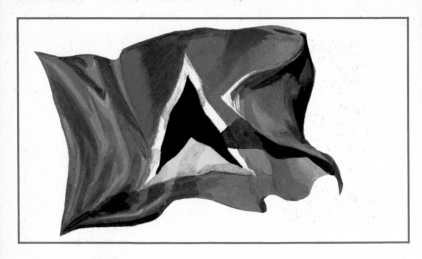

State arms

National flag

St. Lucia, in the Windward Islands (Lesser Antilles), became an associated state of the United Kingdom in 1967 and gained independence in 1979.

The island was discovered by Columbus on St. Lucy's day in 1502. The first attempts to colonize the island (1605 and 1639) met strong resistance from the natives. Subsequently France and Great Britain contended for the island because of its strategic importance. Great Britain finally won out in 1748.

The flag was adopted in 1967. The triangular design stands for the island itself, surrounded by the blue sea. Yellow refers to the island's golden beaches, and black to the island's volcanic origin.

The shield in the coat of arms is divided into quarters by crossed bamboo shoots. Two lilies and two roses are shown in the quarters.

A new national flag was hoisted on October 27, 1979, marking independence for St. Vincent and the Grenadine Islands.

In the center is the coat of arms which had been granted to St. Vincent in 1912. The motto translates as "Peace and Justice," symbolized by two women. The crest is a branch of cotton, an important local crop.

In the flag the coat of arms is set against a breadfruit leaf. St. Vincent was the first island in the Caribbean to grow this important crop after the tree was imported from the Pacific.

The national flag of St. Vincent and the Grenadines was designed by Elaine Liverpool. The narrow white stripes are symbols of purity. The broad stripes of green, yellow, and blue stand, respectively, for fertile vegetation, tropical sunshine, and the sky and sea. St. Vincent had previously been under British colonial domination and flew the Union Jack and other typical colonial flags.

State arms

National flag

209

Barbados

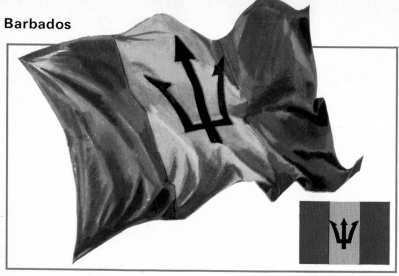

The flag of Barbados, adopted in 1966, was designed by Grantley W. Prescod on the occasion of the state's independence. The island's geographical position is reflected in the design. Blue and gold stand for the sky and sea and the country's golden beaches. All that remains of the trident that appeared in the colonial coat of arms is the upper part in the gold band of the flag.

The state coat of arms dates from 1965.

The *Ficus barbata* (fig tree) gave the island its name. Orchids grow on Barbados. The crest is an arm holding two sugar canes. The supporters are a dolphin and a pelican.

State arms

Governor-general's flag

Prime minister's flag

This small island in the Windwards has been an independent state within the Commonwealth since February 7, 1974.

This unusual flag was hoisted on independence. The nutmeg on the green triangle reflects the importance of this product in the local economy. The seven stars stand for the seven administrative divisions of the state. Red, yellow, and green represent courage, the sun, and agriculture, respectively.

The ship in the center of the shield commemorates Christopher Columbus's landing on the island. The lions in the quarters stand for the island's past and present connections with Great Britain, while the lilies symbolize the Catholic religion.

The state flag and civil ensign differ in size. Their proportions are 3:5 and 1:2, respectively.

Civil ensign

State arms

211

South America

Colombia

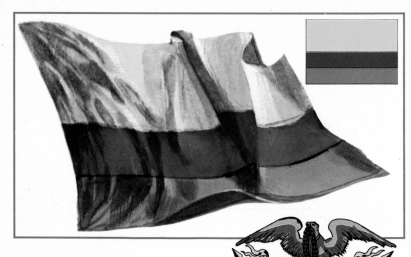

The tricolour designed by Francisco Miranda in 1806 and used by Simón Bolívar was adopted by the Federal Republic of Greater Colombia, which included Colombia, Ecuador, and Venezuela. Bolívar's attempt to create a federation of the states of South America, of which the federal republic represented the first phase, failed in 1830. But Colombia, Ecuador, and Venezuela continued to use the flag. The Colombian version was officially adopted in 1861.

The colours stand for America (yellow), the Atlantic Ocean (blue),

State arms

and Spain (red). The ocean separates the two continents.

The pomegranate on the shield reflects the fact that Colombia was called New Granada until 1861. The pomegranate is the emblem of the Spanish city of Granada. The horns of plenty stand for prosperity, the Phrygian cap for liberty. In the main field the Isthmus of Panama is shown. Until 1903 it was part of Colombia. The condor with the laurel wreath is a symbol of independence.

Presidential flag

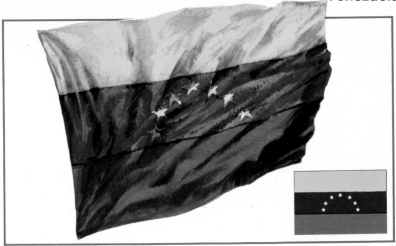

The present version of the Venezuelan flag was adopted in 1930. The colours yellow, blue, and red date to 1806. These colours were subsequently adopted by the Federal Republic of Greater Colombia, which comprised Colombia, Venezuela, and Ecuador. The seven stars, added in 1817, commemorate the country's original provinces.

The horns of plenty in the coat of arms stand for abundance; the wheat sheaf stands for unity and fertility; and the weapons stand for military victories and independence. The wild horse symbolizes liberty.

State arms

State and war ensign and flag

Presidential flag

Netherlands Antilles

State flag

The Netherlands Antilles consist of six Caribbean islands: Curaçao, Aruba, and Bonaire (off the coast of Venezuela), and Saba, St. Eustatius, and part of St. Maarten in the Lesser Antilles. The islands have had self-government since 1954.

The flag dates from 1959. The colours—white, red, and blue—are those of the Dutch flag. The six stars, which also appear in the coat of arms and in the governor's flag, stand for the islands.

State arms

Trinidad and Tobago

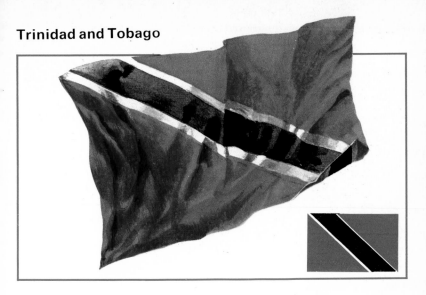

These two islands off the coast of Venezuela have been an independent state within the Commonwealth since 1962. The flag was adopted the same year. Red stands for the generosity of people and for the light of the sun, white for equality and the sea, and black for tenacity and unity. The ship's wheel in the crest of the coat of arms reflects the importance of navigation. On the shield are two humming birds and the three ships of Columbus. The supporters are a red ibis for Trinidad and a *cocorico* for Tobago.

State arms

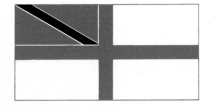

War ensign

Guyana

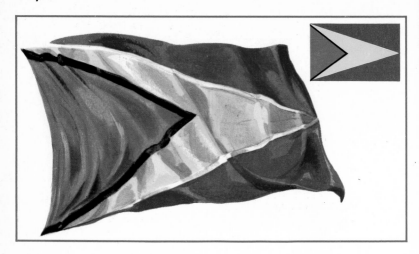

The flag that Guyana adopted in 1966 was designed by Whitney Smith, director of the Flag Research Center of Winchester, Massachusetts. Green stands for agriculture and forests, white for the abundant rivers, and yellow for mineral resources. The energy and zeal of the people in building the new nation are symbolized by the black-edged red triangle. The proportions of the flag are 3:5 on land and 1:2 at sea.

In the crest of the coat of arms are a chieftain's crown and two diamonds. The local fauna and flora are represented by a pheasant and a water lily, the *Victoria regia*. The jaguars hold a pick and a sugar cane.

State arms

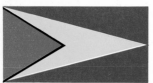

Ensign

Presidential flag

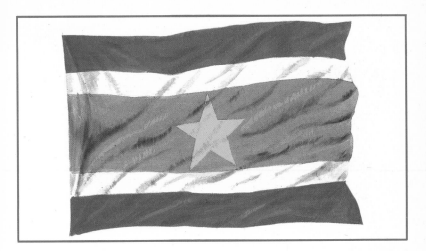

Suriname was ruled by the Netherlands until independence on
November 25, 1975.

The coat of arms dates to the seventeenth century and shows the traditional sailing ship symbolic of commerce. Agriculture is represented by
the palm tree, mining by the diamond
shape in the center of the shield. The
Amerindian population of Suriname,
which still exists, is reflected in the
supporters of the shield. The motto is
in Latin; its meaning is "Justice,
Piety, Faithfulness."

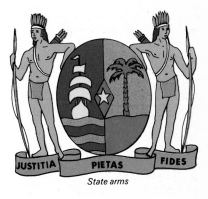

State arms

The national flag replaced an earlier
design at the time of independence.
The star is for unity of the many races
and cultures which coexist in Suriname. Green stands for the fields and
forests of the nation as well as for
hope. Red stands for love and progress,while white is seen as a symbol
of justice and freedom. The yellow
colour of the star is a call for sacrifice,
self-confidence, and altruism on the
part of people so that national progress can be achieved.

National flag

219

Ecuador

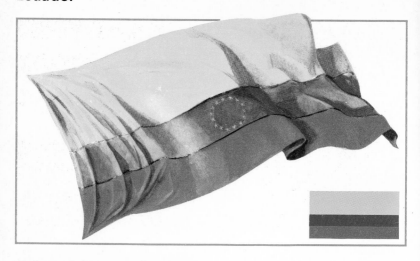

State and war ensign and flag

State arms

Ecuador's colours were used by Ecuador, Colombia, and Venezuela during the wars against Spain in the early 1880s. They were then used by the Federal Republic of Greater Colombia, of which Ecuador was a member. The yellow stands for the sun and natural resources, blue for sky and sea, and red for the blood shed in the defense of the country.

The signs of the zodiac that appear in the coat of arms are those of the period from March to June. It was during those months in 1845 that Ecuador took up arms to defend its freedom. Mount Chimborazo, the highest mountain in the country, is also shown as well as a ship, a symbol of commerce. The condor symbolizes independence, while the bundle of *fasces* stands for republican institutions. On local administrative offices the flag is flown charged with a circle of nineteen white stars on the blue band, symbolizing the nineteen provinces of Ecuador.

220

Provinces of Ecuador

Bolívar

Guayas

Chimborazo

Cañar

Morona Santiago

Azuay

El Oro

Loja

Zamora Chinchipe

Galápagos

Provinces of Ecuador

Esmeraldas

Imbabura

Carchi

Pichincha

Napo

Manabí

Cotopaxi

Tungurahua

Pastaza

Los Rios

222

Peru

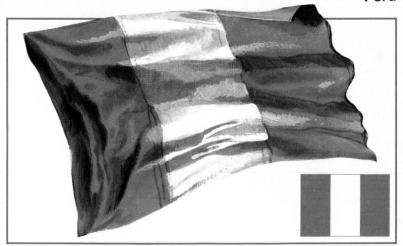

Tradition has it that General José de San Martín selected the colours of the Peruvian flag. In 1820, during the war against Spain, he saw some flamingos with white breasts and red wings take to the air. He is reported to have said, "Those shall be the colours of liberty." Various versions of the flag were used. The present one was officially adopted in 1825.

The llama, the cinchona tree, and the cornucopia in the state coat of arms stand for the fauna, flora, and natural resources of the country. The sun on the president's flag is a traditional Inca symbol.

State arms

Presidential flag
State flag and ensign; war ensign

Brazil

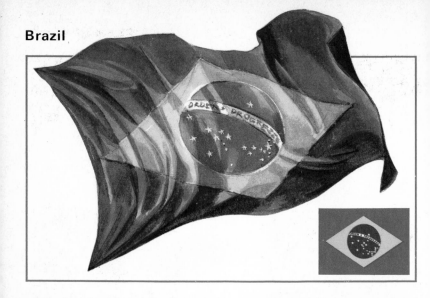

Green and yellow were used as early as the first decades of the nineteenth century to symbolize Brazil's forests and mineral resources (especially gold).

When the republic was established in 1889, the imperial coat of arms was replaced by the celestial globe, which may have been inspired by the armillary globe of the Portuguese flag. The

Presidential flag

State arms

constellations of the Southern Hemisphere are visible on the globe. The stars stand for the twenty-two states and the territories of Brazil. A star is added for every territory that becomes a state. The present version of the flag dates from 1971.

The date on the state emblem is that of the establishment of the republic. The largest star stands for independence and unity. The stars in the center of the blue disk represent the Southern Cross; those in the surrounding ring stand for the states of Brazil. The garland contains tobacco and coffee leaves.

Amazonas

Pará

Piauí

Ceará

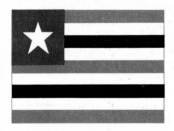

Maranhão

Rio Grande do Norte

Acre

Paraíba

States of Brazil

Pernambuco

Alagôas

Sergipe

Bahía

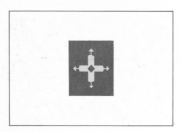

Federal District

Goiás

Espírito Santo

Rio de Janeiro

226

Minas Gerais

São Paulo

Paraná

Mato Grosso

Santa Catarina

Rio Grande do Sul

Mato Grosso do Sul

Chile

State arms

Presidential flag

The Chilean flag, adopted in 1817, was designed by the American Charles Wood, who was a volunteer in the Chilean army. The design is clearly based on that of the United States flag. The colours were used in Chile, however, before the arrival of the Spaniards. Various interpretations of the colours have been given. The most common sees the white as symbolic of the snows of the Andes, the blue as a symbol of the sky, and the red as representing those who have given their lives to defend the country. The star is a symbol of progress and civic virtues.

The coat of arms dates from 1834 and was designed by José Ignacio Zenteno. It repeats the same motifs as the flag. The supporters are a *huemal*, the Andean deer, and a condor. The three feathers of the crest stand for another local animal, the American ostrich.

The motto "By Reason or By Force" was used during the wars of independence.

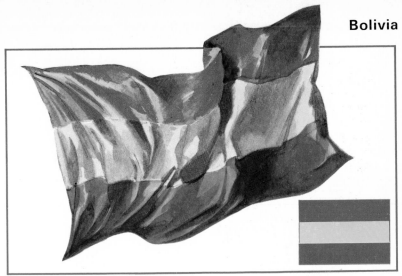

The flag that was adopted in 1888 was the final version of flags used after the proclamation of Bolivia's independence. Red stands for the military valour of the people, yellow for the country's mineral resources, and green for agriculture.

State arms

State and war flag

War ensign

The stars in the state arms stand for the nine departments into which the country is divided. Agriculture and mineral resources are symbolized by wheat and Mount Potosí, where silver is mined. The Phrygian cap is a traditional symbol of liberty. The condor and alpaca represent the local fauna.

Bolivia's hopes of regaining an outlet to the ocean is reflected in the war ensign, which is now only flown on inland waters.

Argentina

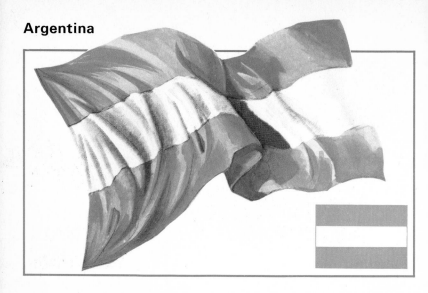

The Argentine flag was adopted in 1816. It had been designed four years earlier by General Manuel Belgrano and was derived from the white and blue cockade that the soldiers of the Liberation Army wore on their uniforms.

The "Sun of May" on the state flag and arms stands for a new age of freedom and for the date May 25, 1810, the day the final struggle for independence began. Six years later Argentina achieved independence.

The Phrygian cap on the emblem is a traditional symbol of liberty and was adopted by several Latin American countries. The clasped hands stand for unity and solidarity.

Presidential flag

State and war flag and ensign

State arms

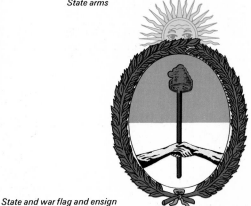

230

Paraguay

The flag of Paraguay was adopted in 1842. It may be based on the red, white, and blue tricolour used in 1812. The flag is unusual in that the state arms appear on the obverse and the treasury seal appears on the reverse.

The star on the state arms, the "Sun of May," refers to the date of independence, May 11, 1811. The treasury seal shows a lion protecting the country's liberty, which is represented by the Phrygian cap.

The president's flag carries the state arms but without the inscription "Republic of Paraguay."

State arms

Treasury seal

Reverse of national flag

Presidential flag

231

Uruguay

The flag of Uruguay was adopted in 1830. The colours and the sun symbol reflect the fact that the country was associated with Argentina until 1828. The white and blue stripes refer to the nine departments into which Uruguay was originally divided. The sun is a symbol of independence.

The present version of the state arms dates from 1908. The scales, the fortress of Montevideo, the horse, and the bull stand for justice, strength, freedom, and abundance, respectively. The oval emblem is framed by olive and laurel branches.

The present jack goes back to 1811 and was Uruguay's first flag.

State arms

Jack

Presidential flag

The Falkland Islands are located about four hundred miles northeast of Cape Horn. Together with South Georgia and the South Sandwich Islands, the Falklands are a British colony. The islands were first sighted by the English navigator John Davis in 1592, and his ship, the *Desire*, is shown in the colony's coat of arms. French settlers arrived in 1764, and English settlers followed a year later. The islands were taken by Spain and annexed to Argentina. In 1833 they were reoccupied by the British.

The coat of arms shows a ship and a ram. The ram stands for the raising of sheep, one of the islands' chief economic resources.

The flag is the British Blue Ensign charged with the colony coat of arms.

State ensign

State arms

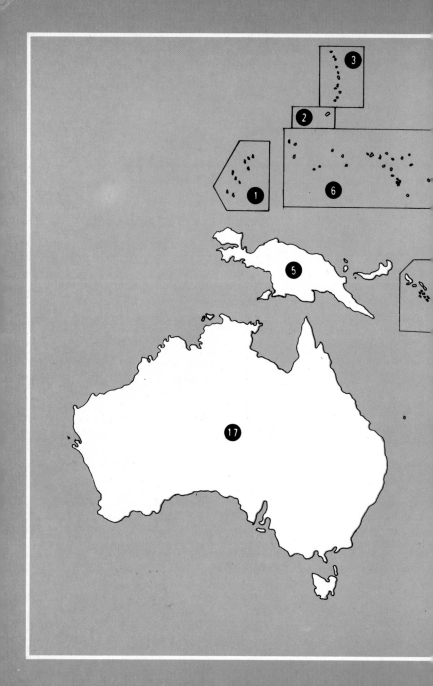

Oceania

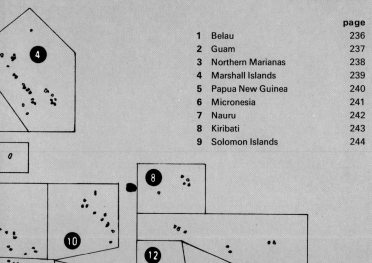

Belau

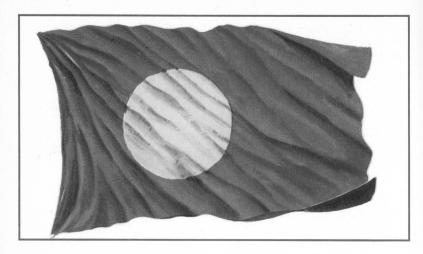

The westernmost part of the former United States Trust Territory of the Pacific Islands became the Republic of Belau on January 1, 1981. The former spelling was Palau.

The national flag of Belau is of very simple design. A golden-yellow disk is set slightly off-center towards the hoist on a field of sky blue. In the flag of Japan, which is similar in design (but not in colours), the disk stands for the sun, but here it symbolizes the moon.

The explanation for the choice of the symbol is found in the history and traditions of the people. It is considered that the full moon is the time for the peak of human activity. Fishing, tree-cutting, planting and harvesting, celebrations, and the carving of canoes are carried on at this time of the month. The moon is therefore a symbol of tranquillity, peace, and love. The blue background symbolizes the transition from foreign domination to self-government.

National flag

Guam

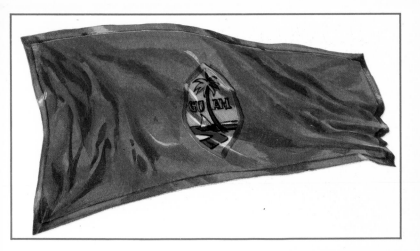

Guam is the largest of the Mariana Islands in the Pacific Ocean. It was probably discovered by the Portuguese navigator Ferdinand Magellan, who called it "Thieves' Island."
Spain claimed Guam in 1565 and kept it until 1898, when it was ceded to the United States as a result of the Spanish-American War. The island was occupied by the Japanese in 1941 and retaken by the United States in 1944. Its position in the Pacific is strategic, and the Americans have a naval base and an air base there with installations for nuclear submarines.
The inhabitants have a large degree of self-government and elect their own governor and legislature.
The flag, which carries the island's emblem, is flown alongside the American flag.

Territorial flag

State seal

Northern Marianas

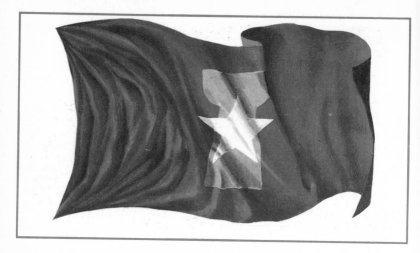

In World War I, Japan seized these islands and ruled them until conquered by American forces in World War II. In 1947 the United Nations recognized a trust territory over the former Japanese possessions, to be administered by the United States. In the course of preparing the islands for self-government, the United States faced opposition to the maintenance of a single government for all the islands. Therefore, in 1976 the Commonwealth of the Northern Marianas was formed as a separate territory.

The flag of the Northern Marianas was first hoisted on July 4, 1976. The blue background represents the Pacific Ocean, the white star the Commonwealth. The silhouette is a grey latte stone reflecting the ancient culture. Such stones were used in the pre-colonial era as underpinnings for the houses of leaders. Many such latte stones still exist and are a distinctive characteristic of the islands.

National flag

When the United States Trust Territory of the Pacific Islands was divided into four parts, the easternmost
group of islands formed a separate
state. The new Marshall Islands government celebrated its inauguration
by the hoisting of a national flag on
May 1, 1979. The flag was designed
by Emlain Kabua; her husband is
president of the Marshall Islands.

National flag

The star over the stripes stands for
the islands, which are a few degrees
above the Equator. The twenty-four
points on the star are for the island
municipalities. The four long rays of
the star suggest the Christian faith of
the country's inhabitants.

White is for brightness, orange for
wealth and bravery. The blue background of the flag is for the Pacific
Ocean. Many other Pacific nations
use flags with stars and/or the
colours blue and white.

Papua New Guinea

State arms

National flag

This state, which became an independent member of the Commonwealth on November 16, 1975, comprises the former New Guinea and the Territory of Papua. New Guinea was once a German possession, then became an Australian trust territory under the League of Nations (1921), and then a United Nations trust territory. Papua had been administered by Australia since 1906. The two areas were united administratively in 1949 and achieved a large measure of self-government in 1973. The flag was adopted officially in 1971 and shows a bird of paradise and the Southern Cross. The Southern Cross is clearly derived from the Australian flag, but it is a common depiction in the flags of Southern Hemisphere countries.

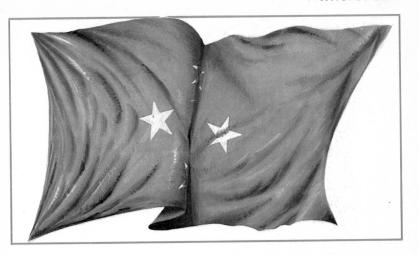

There are three major ethnic divisions of the Pacific Islands—Micronesia, Melanesia, and Polynesia. Micronesia is also a political term, however, referring to the islands under a United Nations trusteeship administered by the United States since the end of World War II. Originally, it was hoped that all the islands could form a single nation at the time of independence.

When various groups of islands decided to form separate nations, the original area of the United States Trust Territory of the Pacific Islands was greatly reduced. A new government was instituted in 1979, and the country was renamed the Federated States of Micronesia. Its flag, adopted by a provisional government in October 1978, resembles the old Trust Territory flag except that there are four stars instead of six. These stand for the member states—Truk, Yap, Ponape, and Kusaie.

The background of the flag is blue, symbolizing the Pacific Ocean. The choice of stars was probably influ-

National flag

enced by their use in the flag of the United States, and the blue may have been suggested by the flag of the United Nations, which is of a similar colour. Full independence has not yet been achieved by the Federated States of Micronesia.

Nauru

This small Pacific island, long an Australian trust territory, obtained independence in 1968.

The flag is symbolic of the island's geographical position. There is a yellow stripe on a blue field. Below the stripe and towards the hoist is a white twelve-pointed star. The island is one degree below the Equator and

National flag

east of the international date line. The twelve points of the star stand for the twelve indigenous tribes of the island.

The star also appears on the coat of arms. The shield is surrounded by coconut-palm leaves and shows the chemical symbol for phosphorus. Phosphates are the island's main source of revenue. There is also a frigate bird and a branch of *tomano*.

State arms

Although its land area and population are small, Kiribati consists of islands spread over a vast area of the Pacific Ocean. These include the Gilbert Islands, "*Ki*-ri-bass" being the local way of pronouncing "Gilberts."

The territory was long under British protection, and the flag and coat of arms are based on the heraldic traditions of Great Britain. The blue and white wavy stripes represent the Pacific Ocean. Above the rising sun is a flying frigate bird, typical of local wildlife. The motto in the coat of arms proclaims "Well-Being and Peace and Prosperity."

Previously Kiribati was politically associated with the Ellice Islands to the south. They were separated legally in 1975 and administratively the following year. In 1978 the Ellice Islands became the independent nation of Tuvalu, and on July 12, 1979, Kiribati attained its sovereignty.

National flag

State arms

Solomon Islands

State arms

National flag on land

When independence was achieved by the Solomon Islands on July 7, 1978, after decades of British rule, a new coat of arms was granted. Its colours are those of the national flag, while its symbols stand for the various districts—frigate birds (Eastern District), the *sandfordi* eagle (Malaita District), two turtles (Western District), and a dancing shield, bow, and arrow (Central District). A Solomon Islands boat, a saltwater crocodile, a shark, and a rising sun complete the design.

The national flag was granted on November 18, 1977, by Queen Elizabeth in anticipation of independence. The blue, yellow, and green stand for water, the sun, and the land, respectively. Stars are characteristic of many Pacific island flags. Here they stand for the Eastern, Western, Malaita, Central, and Eastern Outer Islands Districts of which the country is composed.

The College of Arms in London was responsible for the design of the coat of arms of Tuvalu, based on a concept by R. P. Turner. The location of the islands in the Pacific is suggested by the wavy stripes of gold and blue. Above them is a representation of the traditional meeting house (*maneapa*) of the Tuvalu people. The eight banana leaves and eight seashells, emblems of the fertility of the land, refer to the eight inhabited islands. The motto translates as "Tuvalu for God."

The name Tuvalu means "eight islands" because eight of the nine islands in the national territory are inhabited. All nine of the islands are symbolized by the stars on the national flag. The design, by Vione Natano, was hoisted on Independence Day, October 1, 1978. The Union Jack in the canton (upper hoist corner) suggests close links between Tuvalu and Great Britain.

State arms

National flag

Vanuatu

Independent on July 30, 1980, the Republic of Vanuatu introduced a new national flag and coat of arms.

The coat of arms shows a mountain, a Melanesian warrior in traditional costume, a ribbon with the national motto, "We Stand With God" in Bislama, a form of Pidgin English.

The national emblem, the tusk of a pig surmounted by crossed *namele* leaves, is symbolic of national riches, the leaves are a reminder of the traditional way of life of the people. This national emblem also appears on the national flag on a black triangle, standing both for the rich soil of the country and for the Melanesian people. The yellow capital Y, recalling that the islands of Vanuatu are in the shape of a Y, stands for peace and the light of Christianity.

The other stripes of the flag are red and green. The former recalls the blood of sacrificial pigs and the power of custom, as well as human blood and the unity of all people in the country. The bottom stripe is green, signifying the islands of Vanuatu. The flag was designed by Kalontas Malon and modified by Rick Fraser, who created the design of the Vanuatu coat of arms.

State arms

Western Samoa was a trust territory administered by New Zealand until it achieved independence within the Commonwealth in 1962.

The flag was officially adopted in 1949 (a year after a version with four stars had been approved). The main element of the flag is the constellation of the Southern Cross, which appears in several other flags of the Southern Hemisphere.

White, blue, and red stand for purity, freedom, and courage, respectively.

In the state coat of arms, the cross represents the Christian faith, as does the motto "May God Be the Foundation of Samoa." The olive branches are a symbol of peace. The palm tree also appeared in the colonial coat of arms.

National flag

State arms

American Samoa

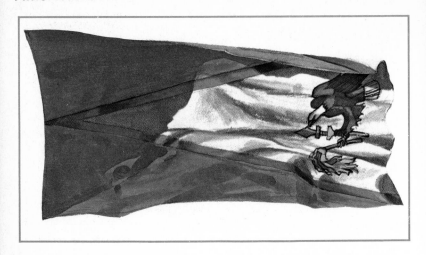

State seal

The first European to visit the Samoan archipelago in the Pacific Ocean was the Dutchman J. Roggeveen in 1722. Eastern Samoa has been an American dependency since 1899, and there is a United States naval base there. The territory is administered by the governor, with a senate and a house of representatives.

The kingdom of Samoa and the United States reached an agreement in 1878, when America wanted to check German expansion in the Pacific.

The flag has been in use since 1960. It shows an American eagle with the staff of a chief and a war club, symbols of authority.

Territorial flag

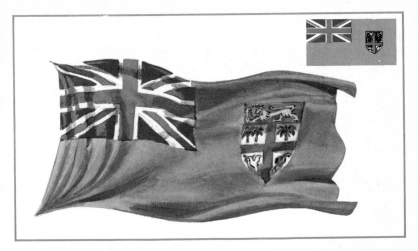

The Fiji Islands have been an independent member of the Commonwealth since 1970. The flag reflects the islands' long connection with Great Britain. The coat of arms shows the British lion and the St. George's cross as well as sugar cane, coconuts, a dove of peace, and a bunch of bananas. An outrigger canoe and the motto "Fear God and Honour the King" also appear in the coat of arms.

Civil ensign

War ensign

State ensign

State arms

Tonga

Tonga, or the Friendly Islands, became an independent kingdom within the Commonwealth in 1970.

The population is Christian, and the red cross in the flag refers to the blood of Christ. The state coat of arms also shows a red cross as well as a dove of peace.

Other symbols in the coat of arms are three stars for the three main groups of islands, a crown for the monarchy, and three swords that do homage to the three dynasties that have ruled the islands. The motto can be translated as "God and Tonga Are My Heritage."

State arms

National flag

Royal flag

250

Cook Islands

The Cook Islands are located in the South Pacific some 1,800 miles northeast of New Zealand. In 1595 the Spanish navigator Alvaro de Mendaña became the first European to sight them. Captain James Cook, for whom the islands are named, visited them several times between 1773 and 1777. They became a British protectorate in 1888 and were annexed to New Zealand in 1901. Since 1965 the islands have been largely self-governing. The local population is culturally similar to the Maoris of New Zealand.

National flag on land

While awaiting full independence, the Cook Islands have adopted a flag with fifteen white stars arranged in a circle on a blue field under the Union Jack. The stars stand for the islands of the archipelago, and the Union Jack is a reminder of Commonwealth associations.

Australia

The first Australian national flag was hoisted in 1901 and was almost identical with the one that was approved by Queen Elizabeth II when she visited the country in 1954.

The flag is the British Blue Ensign charged with six white stars. The seven points of the star that appears below the Union Jack stand for the six states and the territories that form the Commonwealth of Australia. The other five stars represent the Southern Cross.

The supporters in the coat of arms are Australia's national animals, the kangaroo and the emu. The crest is a more elaborate version of the Commonwealth star of the flag. The quarters of the shield show emblems of the Australian states: a St. George's cross charged with a lion and four stars for New South Wales; a crown and the Southern Cross for Victoria; a Maltese cross for Queensland; a shrike for South Australia; a black swan for Western Australia; and a lion for Tasmania.

State arms

Australia

Civil ensign (alternate)

War ensign

National flag on land; jack; civil ensign (alternate)

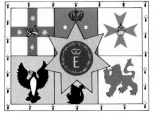

Queen Elizabeth's personal flag for Australia

Australian states and territories

New South Wales

Queensland

Western Australia

South Australia

Australian states and territories

Victoria

Tasmania

Norfolk Island

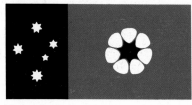

Northern Territory

Norfolk Island features its distinctive local pine tree on its flag, while Sturt's desert rose appears in the Northern Territory's flag. The ochre and black of the latter are colours common in the art of Northern Territory Aborigines.

New Zealand

New Zealand has been an independent member of the Commonwealth since 1931. In 1902 it had already adopted a variation of the British Blue Ensign charged with four stars representing the constellation of the Southern Cross.

The coat of arms shows the Southern Cross (standing for New Zealand itself) as well as symbols of commerce (the ships), agriculture, and industry. The supporters are a European woman and a Maori warrior.

State arms

War ensign

Civil ensign

Queen Elizabeth's personal flag for New Zealand

255

International Flags

International organizations—for defense, assistance, and mutual aid—have also adopted flags, especially in the period following World War II.

The symbolism of these flags is generally much more specific than that of national flags. The Red Cross and the Red Crescent are specifically religious symbols in origin, and these two parallel organizations are devoted to humanitarian activities. The flags of the Olympic Games symbolize international harmony and the hope of peace between nations. Other flags, like that of the Arab League, are also specific in their symbolism. The green of the Arab League flag is a universal symbol of Islam.

International Red Cross

This flag was adopted at the 1863 meeting of the International Committee of the Red Cross. The Red Cross was originally established to provide aid to casualties in time of war, but since then its humanitarian activities have been extended to peacetime assistance as well. The Swiss flag, with the colours reversed, provided the model for the organization's flag.

The Red Crescent

This is the Muslim equivalent of the Red Cross. The crescent is a traditional Islamic Symbol.

Red Lion and Sun

For many years a distinctive centuries-old national symbol, the lion and sun, was used by the Iranian organization associated with the Geneva Convention. Following the revolution in 1979 in Iran, that symbol was replaced by the red crescent used by other Muslim countries. Thus, although it still is legally in existence, the Red Lion and Sun flag is no longer in actual use.

United Nations

This flag was adopted by the General Assembly on October 20, 1947. The blue field is charged with the organization's emblem. The worldwide nature of the UN and its mission of peace are expressed by the two olive branches embracing the globe.

Olympic Games

This flag was created in 1913 at the suggestion of Baron Pierre de Coubertin, the founder of the modern Olympics. The flag was first flown at the Antwerp games in 1920. The five rings represent the five continents brought together in the fraternal spirit of the Olympic Games.

Council of Europe

The Council of Europe was established in 1949 to promote political, economic, and cultural cooperation among its member nations. In 1953 the council adopted a flag with fifteen stars. The number was reduced to twelve in 1955.

International Flags

North Atlantic Treaty Organization (NATO)

The North Atlantic Treaty Organization was established in 1949 to defend the member states of the Atlantic Pact. The flag was flown for the first time on October 28, 1953. Blue stands for the Atlantic Ocean, while the circle and compass express the unity and peace-keeping mission of the alliance.

Arab League

The Arab League was established on March 22, 1945 to promote the political and economic development of the Arab nations. Green symbolizes the Islamic faith of the member nations, and the chain stands for unity.

East African Community (EAC)

This organization was founded in 1967 by Kenya, Uganda, and Tanzania to develop economic and political cooperation, but has since been dissolved. The three stars stood for the member states.

Organization of American States (OAS)

This association of North, Central, and South American states was founded in Rio de Janeiro in 1947. Its aims are mutual defense and the economic and social development of member countries. The flags of the member states are shown in the organization flag.

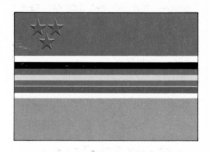

Organization of Central American States

This organization was founded in San Salvador in 1951. The member states are Nicaragua, Guatemala, Costa Rica, El Salvador, and Honduras; and their aim is political, military, and economic cooperation.
The five volcanoes in the emblem stand for the member nations. The Phrygian cap and the triangle are common symbols in Latin America.

Colombo Plan

The Colombo Plan was established in 1950. The industrial countries— Canada, the United States, Great Britain, Japan, New Zealand, and Australia—provide technical assistance to Southern and Southeast Asian countries.
The cogwheel and the ears of grain stand for the kinds of assistance provided by the plan.

Southeast Asia Treaty Organization (SEATO)

This military alliance was established in 1954 with the cooperation of France, Great Britain, the United States, Pakistan, New Zealand, Thailand, Australia, and the Philippines.
The defensive aims of the organization, now dissolved, were symbolized by the white shield and the olive branch.

Glossary

Banner—A flag, especially one of heraldic design or elegant manufacture.

Base—The lower portion of the shield in a coat of arms.

Bearing—See *Charge*.

Canton—A square or rectangular section of a flag or shield. The canton of a flag is usually in the upper left corner next to the staff. The canton of a shield is in the same position.

Charge—Any figure, symbol, or emblem on the field of a flag or shield.

Civil flag; civil ensign—See *Flag; Ensign*.

Coat of arms—Emblems and figures forming the symbolic insignia of a nation, a city, or an organization, or a family. The main elements of a coat of arms are the shield, the crest, wreath, helmet, supporters, compartment, and motto.

Cockade—A badge in the form of a ribbon rosette; a very popular political emblem in the nineteenth century.

Colours—A country's flag

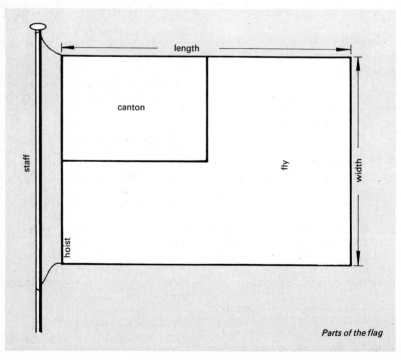

Parts of the flag

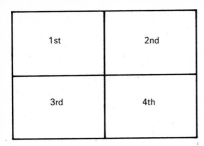

Quarters of the flag

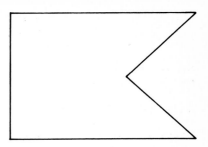

Swallow – tailed flag

(figuratively); specifically, the flag of a military unit. In heraldry the recognized colours are sable (black), azure (blue), gules (red), vert (green), and purpure (purple), and are distinguished from the metals—argent (silver) and / or (gold) – and furs.

Compartment—The sustaining base for a shield and its supporters in a coat of arms.

Crest—The heraldic symbol above the wreath in a coat of arms. It may also be shown separately.

Emblem—Some nations have adopted a symbol, often of heraldic origin, to be used instead of a coat of arms. It may be used separately or as a charge on a flag.

Ensign—A national flag displayed on a ship. Privately owned craft fly the civil ensign, while battleships use the war ensign. Unarmed government vessels fly the state ensign.

Field—The background colour of a flag or shield.

Flag—A piece of cloth, of variable shape but usually rectangular, normally attached by its short side to a staff. It bears the colours and symbols of a nation, city, corporation, etc. Aside from its use for identification or recognition, a national flag is above all a symbol of significant political content. Private citizens fly the civil flag, public buildings use the state flag; the armed forces may have a special war flag.

Fly—The outer edge of a flag; also the distance from the staff to the outer edge.

Gonfalon—A swallow-tailed flag hanging from a horizontal bar attached to a staff. It was used especially by medieval Italian communes, the Catholic Church, and other organizations.

Greek cross—A cross with four equal arms.

Half-mast—The hanging of a flag below the top of the flagstaff, in sign of mourning.

Helmet—The part of the coat of arms between the wreath and the shield.

Glossary

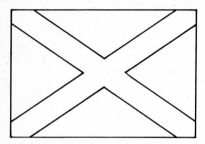

Saltire (St. Andrew's cross)

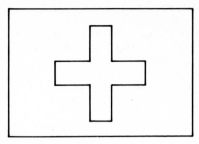

Cross couped (Greek cross)

Hoist—The measurement of a flag along the staff; also the area of the flag nearest the staff.

Jack—A flag flown at the bow of a ship, indicating nationality.

Length—The measurement of a flag at right angles to the staff.

Mantling—The stylized representation in a coat of arms of the cloth which hung from the top of a knight's helmet, originally designed to protect the wearer from heat and dirt.

Merchant flag—See *Ensign*.

Obverse—The more important side of a flag is the one visible when the flagstaff is to the left of the observer.

Proportions—The relative width and length of a flag, e.g. 2 : 3.

Quarter—An area of a shield or flag obtained by dividing the field with horizontal and vertical lines.

Reverse—The less important side of a flag, usually the one visible when the flagstaff is to the right of the observer.

St Andrew's cross—An X-shaped cross

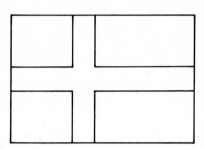

Scandinavian cross

Quarters of the shield

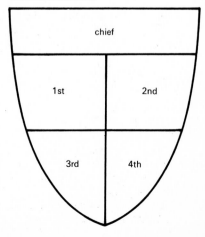

262

Saltire—See *St. Andrew's cross.*

Scandinavian cross—A cross with the vertical arms closer to the staff of the flag.

Staff—The metal or wood mast that is used to support a flag.

Standard—A flag of heraldic or military origin that is highly visible and usually represents a head of state or other leader.

State flag; state ensign—See *Flag; Ensign.*

Supporters—Human or animal figures that appear at the sides of a shield in a coat of arms.

Swallow tail—The fly end of a flag from which a triangular portion has been cut; used especially in Scandinavian countries.

Vexillology—The scientific study of flag history and symbolism.

War flag; war ensign—See *Flag; Ensign.*

Width—The measurement of a flag made along the staff side.

Wreath—The silk braid depicted in a coat of arms between the crest and the helmet.

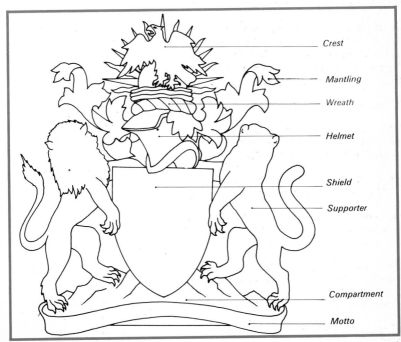

Crest

Mantling

Wreath

Helmet

Shield

Supporter

Compartment

Motto

Parts of coat of arms

Index

Index

Index

Index

Index

Index

Bibliography

The Flag Bulletin; a bimonthly journal dealing with all aspects of flags, published since 1961 by the Flag Research Center (Winchester, Mass. 01890).

The Flag Book of the United States by Whitney Smith (New York: Morrow, revised edition, 1975); the standard reference on all aspects of American flag history and usage.

Flags Through the Ages and Across the World by Whitney Smith (New York: McGraw-Hill, 1975); the most comprehensive book on the subject.

Flags and Arms Across the World by Whitney Smith (New York: McGraw-Hill, 1980).

National Flags of the World (Winchester, Mass.; Flag Research Center); a wall chart regularly updated.

Flags of the World by E.M.C. Barraclough and William Crampton (London: Warne; revised edition, 1981).

What So Proudly We Hail by William Furlong (Washington, D.C.: Smithsonian Institution, 1981).